LEARN TO SUCCEED

For Janie, Rosa and Christina

"Wealth is the means and people are the ends. All our material riches will avail us little if we do not use them to expand the opportunities of our people." (J.F. Kennedy)

LEARN TO SUCCEED

The case for a skills revolution

Mike Campbell

The POLICY PRESS

First published in Great Britain in May 2002 by

The Policy Press
34 Tyndall's Park Road
Bristol BS8 1PY
UK

Tel +44 (0)117 954 6800
Fax +44 (0)117 973 7308
e-mail tpp@bristol.ac.uk
www.policypress.org.uk

British Library Cataloguing in Publication Data
A catalogue record for this book is available from the British Library

ISBN 1 86134 269 1 paperback
A hardcover version of this book is also available

Mike Campbell is Director of Policy and Research at the Sector Skills Development Agency.

Cover design by Qube Design Associates, Bristol.
Front cover: photograph kindly supplied by www.johnbirdsall.co.uk

Printed and bound in Great Britain by Bell & Bain Ltd, Glasgow

Contents

List of tables and figures

Tables

Figures

Preface and acknowledgements

This book provides an evidence-based argument for the pursuit of a more highly skilled society. It argues that raising skill levels is vital to both economic success and social inclusion. In short it argues that we need to learn, in order that we may succeed. It sets out the arguments and evidence on the value of education and training. It provides a succinct account of the available evidence on the stock of the nation's skills and the changing demand for them. It provides a foundation stone for policy development, for the setting of priorities and for action, to turn our relatively 'skill poor' country into a 'skill rich' country. It provides material that should assist policy makers and practitioners in encouraging people and business that they do, indeed, need to 'learn to succeed'.

Over the last six or seven years, I have made over 100 presentations at conferences, seminars, workshops, dinners and other events on this theme. I have also worked on skills issues, with my colleagues here at the Policy Research Institute, on around 50 research projects for local and regional agencies (Regeneration Partnerships, Training and Enterprise Councils, Learning and Skills Councils, Learning Partnerships, government offices in the regions, Regional Development Agencies); for national government departments (most notably, of course, the Department for Education and Skills); and for international agencies (the European Commission and the Organisation for Economic Co-operation and Development). I recently undertook a review of the economic benefits of learning for the National Advisory Council on the Education and Training Targets (Campbell, 2000) and also had the privilege of working with the National Skills Task Force as a member of its research group (NSTF, 2000). I was also a member of the research group advising the Cabinet Office on workforce development. I have also recently completed, with colleagues in the Policy Research Institute, an assessment of the state of skills in England (Campbell et al, 2001). It is time, therefore, that an attempt was made to draw on this material and experience to provide what the author believes is a much needed synthesis of 'the case for skills'.

I am very grateful to the many organisations who have commissioned the Policy Research Institute to work on these themes over the years and, in particular, to the Department for Education and Skills. I am also grateful to my colleagues here who have worked with me on these projects – in particular Simon Baldwin, Steve Johnson, Ben Mitchell, Alexandra Upton and Fiona Walton. I am also indebted to my secretary, Helen Burns, who once again has borne the burden of word processing the text. Ben Mitchell prepared the list of references. Thanks are also due to Professor Ian Stone of the Northern Economic Research Unit at the University of Northumbria who read an earlier version of the typescript and offered a series of helpful suggestions.

This book provides argument and evidence. It is, however, not enough. Political will and institutional capacity are both also required to drive through the necessary change. If the reader needs convincing of the importance, and difficulty, of so doing then read Robert Reich's superb account of his four years spent trying to engineer a skills revolution in the US as Secretary of Labour in President Clinton's first administration (Reich, 1998). The challenge is indeed great, but then so is the prize.

Mike Campbell
Leeds
December 2001

ONE

Introduction: skills for all

"Upon the education of the people of this country, the fate of our people depends." (Disraeli)

This book argues that raising skill levels is crucial to both economic success and social inclusion. It shows that the UK, despite substantial progress in recent years, has a number of serious skills deficiencies. At the same time it shows that the need for skills is great, and increasing, and that there are significant benefits which are likely to accrue to people, companies and the community at large, through raising skill levels. It sets out the barriers that need to be overcome to effectively tackle skills deficiencies and proposes an agenda of what needs to be done in order to create a highly skilled, prosperous and inclusive society.

The skills agenda is at the heart of many of the current government's policy priorities. It is not, however, the purpose of this book to describe, review or assess such policies. In itself this would be a considerable undertaking. Instead, the book makes the economic case for a skills agenda, synthesising a wide range of argument and evidence in a convenient form that is accessible to practitioners and policy makers as well as to students and academics. Necessarily, the arguments and evidence are condensed. However, readers are referred to the references indicated in the text if they should require a more intensive treatment of specific issues.

The rest of the chapter proceeds, firstly, by providing a brief indication of the competitiveness and social exclusion problems, to whose resolution an upgrading of workforce skills can contribute so much; and secondly, by dealing with some terminology and definitions used throughout the book.

The economic challenge

The UK economy is one of the largest and richest in the world. Nevertheless we are faced with a number of important challenges. First, in terms of overall living standards we can assess the UK's relative position in terms of Gross Domestic Product (GDP) per head (DTI, 2001). Indeed, GDP per head is also often thought of as the best single measure of a country's competitive position. GDP per head in the UK, in 1999, was around £23,000 (at purchasing power parity), which therefore ranks the UK 16th in terms of the 29 Organisation for Economic Co-operation and Development (OECD) countries. This is fractionally above both the OECD and EU averages and countries such as Spain, France, Greece, Poland and Mexico but below, for example, Norway, Iceland, Australia and Ireland; as well as more familiar competitor countries such as the USA, Japan and Germany. Overall, GDP per head is 21% below the average of the G7 countries (our major competitors). We can reasonably say that living standards and competitiveness have both some way to go to catch up with 'the best'.

Second, the UK has a weak productivity performance (DTI, 2001; HM Treasury, 2001) – this is important, because productivity growth is the most important determinant of long-term GDP growth. Labour productivity is below that in all G7 countries, except Japan, and is 'significantly' below the OECD and EU averages. Measured by output per worker the 'productivity gap' amounts to over 40% with the US, nearly 20% with France and over 10% with Germany (see Figure 1.1 below). If the UK were able to match the productivity performance of the US, output per head would be £6,000 higher.

Furthermore, four fifths of the labour input to economic growth in recent years (1986-99) came from the increasing skills of the labour force rather than the increased size of the employed labour force.

Moreover, within the UK, there are enormous differences in the productivity performance of different plants. For example, in terms of Gross Value Added (GVA) per worker, the most productive plants are up to five-and-a-half times as productive as the least productive. Even within the same sector the gap varies from around three-and-a-half times to six times. It is estimated that the gaps are even wider in the service sectors of the economy. Furthermore, the most productive plants are, overall, the most highly skilled plants. For example, plants in the two higher productivity quartiles both have higher ratios of skilled to unskilled workers than the lowest two quartiles (HM Treasury, 2001).

Figure 1.1: The productivity gap (GDP per worker, UK = 100)

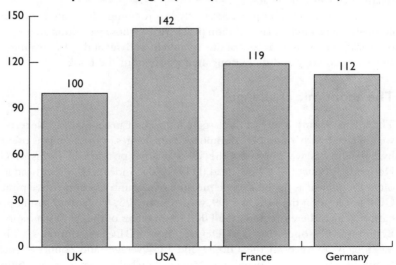

Source: HM Treasury (2001, Chart 1.3)

The social challenge

Turning now to social inclusion, there is a range of 'economic' dimensions to social inclusion which are potentially able to be influenced by skills issues, as they relate to (un)employment and income. We identify six such dimensions (Percy-Smith, 2000; DWP, 2001):

• 16% of all children under the age of 16 live in 'workless' households;
• 12% of the entire population of working age live in workless households;
• 32% of all children live in households where income levels are less than 60% of the national median income – in effect living in 'poverty';
• 18% of working age adults live in households where income levels are less than 60% of the national median income;
• while 74% of adults of working age are in employment, only 67% of those aged over 50 are; only 49% of lone parents and 57% of people from minority ethnic communities;
• there is an extensive concentration of workless households, low-income households, low employment rates and other dimensions of economic exclusion in a range of localities and neighbourhoods in the UK (Social Exclusion Unit, 1998).

If enhancing skill levels can have an impact on increasing the prospects of many of these people's earnings and employment opportunities, it would make a substantial contribution to tackling social exclusion.

A framework for skills assessment

Figure 1.2(a) provides a framework within which to examine skills issues and to become acquainted with the terminology used in the book and we now consider its main elements in turn. Learning, education and training are seen as activities or *processes* through which skills are acquired. They are, if you like, the inputs to skill formation. Participation in such learning can lead to successful *outcomes*. The outcomes from this process of learning are ultimately a set of skills – competencies, proficiencies, the ability to do something effectively – which have been acquired through the learning undertaken. Often the learning leads to *qualifications* or some other form of certification which demonstrates that the individual has performed successfully to a certain level. Throughout the book we refer to such qualification levels in terms of NVQ 'equivalents'. The main qualifications related to these levels are broadly as shown in Table 1.1.

Additionally, or alternatively to acquiring qualifications, people develop a technical or practical competence associated with their job or they may enter or progress through, *occupations*. These are jobs which are officially classified according to their content and skill levels, such as in the Standard Occupational Classification (SOC). A range of other competencies may be developed or acquired, which can be utilised across a range of different occupations and, as such, are 'transferable'. These *generic* skills encompass numeracy and literacy,

Figure 1.2(a): A framework for skills assessment – Part 1

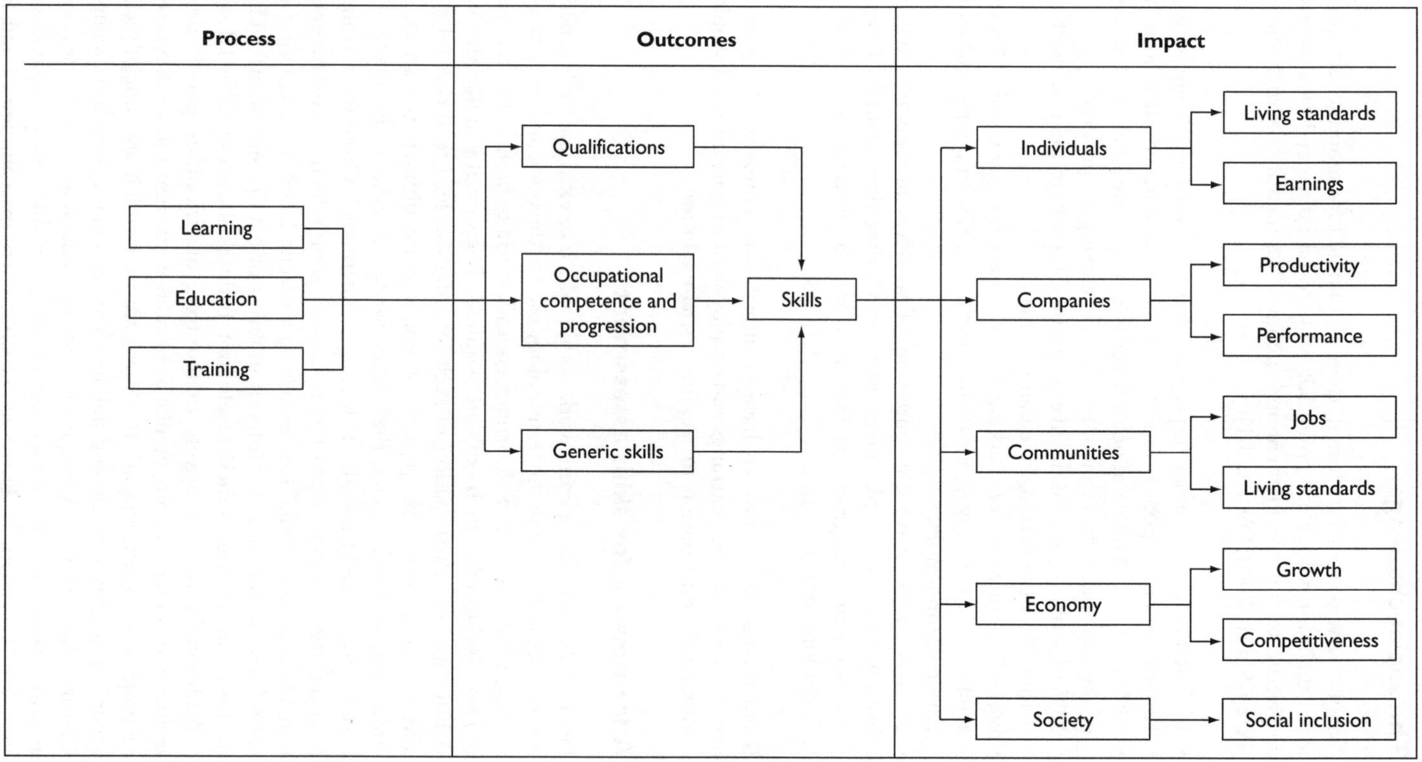

Table 1.1: NVQ levels and equivalent qualifications

NVQ level	Qualification
5	Higher Degree; Professional Qualifications
4	First Degree; Teaching Qualification; Nursing Qualification; HNC/HND; RSA Higher Diploma; some Professional Qualifications
3	2 or more 'A' (Advanced) Levels; RSA Advanced Diploma; ONC/OND; National BTEC; City and Guilds Advanced Craft; Trade Apprenticeship; Advanced GNVQ
2	5 or more GCSEs at Level A-C; 1 'A' (Advanced) Level; GNVQ Intermediate; RSA Diploma; City and Guilds Craft; BTEC General
1	Less than 5 GCSEs at Level A-C; GNVQ

Information and Communication Technology skills, problem solving, team working, verbal and written communication and so on. Both occupational progression and acquisition of generic skills may, or may not, be formally certificated.

We generally use qualifications and occupations as 'proxies' for the measurement of skill. This is very useful as it makes otherwise heterogeneous skills comparable. However, they are only proxies. People may develop their skills in ways that cannot easily be picked up by these proxies and the content of both occupations and qualifications can change over time. On occasion in this book we therefore identify other dimensions of skills – employees own assessment of skill levels, and whether these are increasing or decreasing; as well as employers' assessment of the skills of their workforce or the people they recruit to join them. Skills are, in the end, the competencies that are actually deployed on the job and are very difficult to measure and make comparable. Many of these may be 'learnt' through experience and take the form of 'tacit' knowledge.

The *impact* of acquiring these skills is very important to the focus and argument of this book. Do these acquired skills actually improve people's earnings, their employability and employment prospects? Are they connected to the evolving needs of the labour market? Do these skills, when acquired, enhance the competitive performance of the businesses for whom they work or, if a public or not-for-profit organisation, do they improve the services provided to users? Do communities with higher skill levels secure more and better jobs and enjoy higher levels of economic wellbeing? Does the economy become more competitive? Does it grow faster? Does society become a more equitable, inclusive place in which to live? These are enormous questions that can, of course, only partially and provisionally be answered – both in this book, and more generally, given our current state of knowledge. Nonetheless, for there to be a sound economic case for skills acquisition it is necessary to be able to demonstrate a positive impact of skills on many of these phenomena.

However, if we are to *fully* examine and assess the skills agenda we have to go beyond examining the outcomes from learning activity and the benefits that accrue to people, companies and the wider community and economy in order to examine some further aspects of skill issues which are summarised in Figure 1.2(b). First, are the outcomes from learning appropriate to labour market

Figure 1.2(b): A framework for skills assessment – Part 2

Deficiencies	Imbalances	Inequalities	Barriers	Priorities
Level and structure of skills – supply deficiencies	Skill shortages Skill surpluses	The distribution of skills – social groups geography	Market failures	Make the case for skills Progression Participation Skill hotspots
Skill requirements	Skill gaps		Other barriers	Employer action
Demand deficiencies International comparisons	Latent skill gaps			Geographical inequalities Social inequalities International benchmarking

requirements? Is the supply of skills that is made available suitable, adequate or sufficient? Are there any problems in respect of the structure or composition of the supply? How do skill levels compare with other countries? In sum, are there *supply deficiencies*. Second, how are the skills that are actually demanded changing over time? Is there evidence of increasing skill requirements? How far are these demands influenced by broader business strategy? In sum, are there *demand deficiencies*? Third, as a result of the interaction between the skills supply and skills demand conditions, what are the nature of any *skill imbalances* that have arisen between the two in the form of shortages, gaps or surpluses? Fourth, how are such skills distributed across the population? How evenly distributed are these skills across social groups? To what extent are they unevenly distributed geographically? In other words what are the *inequalities* associated with skills issues. Fifth, to the extent that there exist deficiencies, imbalances, and inequalities, what are the *barriers* that prevent people and organisations from increasing their skill levels and realising the benefits of skill acquisition? And, finally, based on all of this, what are the main *priorities for action* to raise skill levels?

This book seeks to address these issues in our assessment of the 'state of skills'.

The rest of the book proceeds as follows. Chapter Two examines the UK skills position in terms of the skills we have available. Chapter Three then assesses changing skill needs while Chapter Four considers the 'value' of skills. Chapter Five concludes by setting an agenda for action, identifying key skill priorities and the barriers we need to overcome in order to pursue them effectively.

TWO

What skills have we got?

"Human history becomes more and more a race between education and catastrophe." (H.G.Wells)

This chapter examines the supply of skills: the skills that are currently available in the UK. First, we will consider the overall level of skills in the workforce as well as the situation of both young people and adults; and we shall examine how these skills have been changing over recent years. Second, we will go on to assess the nature and extent of the inequalities that exist in workforce qualifications between different social groups as well as the problem of basic skills. Third, we review the participation of both young people and adults in learning (including training) and consider some of the barriers which prevent higher levels of participation from occuring. Next, we outline the skills of both the unemployed and the economically inactive before moving on to consider the problems of the existence of skills shortages and skills gaps. Finally, the chapter seeks to place UK skill levels in international context by benchmarking our skills position and recent performance against that of other OECD countries.

Workforce qualifications

Overall, around one quarter of the workforce (27%) are qualified to NVQ level 4 and above; a quarter (25%) to NVQ level 3 and above; and a fifth (23%) to NVQ level 2 or above. Around 14% are qualified to NVQ level 1 while about 11% have no recognised qualifications at all (see Figure 2.1). These figures represent a considerable improvement from the situation that existed 20 years ago. In 1979 more than 40% of the economically active did not hold any qualifications (compared to 15% today) and only just over 20% were qualified to NVQ level 3 or above (compared to 48% today).

More recent change demonstrates the continuing shift towards a more highly qualified workforce. Since 1995 there has been a reduction in the proportion of the economically active whose highest qualification is below level 2 and an increase in the proportion qualified to NVQ or equivalent levels 2, 3 and 4+ (see Figure 2.1). Between 1995 and 2001, the number of economically active people increased by approximately 700,000 but the increase in the numbers of those qualified to NVQ level 3 and above amounted to around one-and-a-half million. More than one million of these were qualified to NVQ level 4. On the other hand there was a decrease of more than one million in the numbers of those without any qualifications

Figure 2.1: Highest NVQ equivalent qualification held by economically active population, England (1995-2001, %)

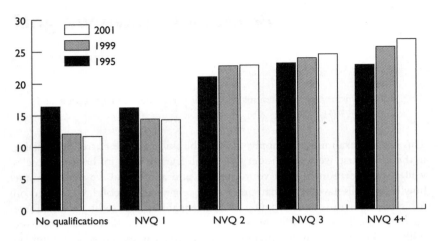

Source: Labour Force Survey (1995, 1999, 2001)

This situation can be unpicked a little by examining, in turn, the qualifications of young people and adults. Currently 75% of *young people* reach NVQ level 2 or equivalent by age 19. There has been significant progress in recent years with regard to the proportion of young people qualified to level 2. The proportion qualified to level 2 has increased from 63% in 1993 – an increase of nearly a fifth. This is in large part due to the increased proportion of young people obtaining five higher grade (A–C) GCSEs – 49% of 16–year-olds obtained such qualifications in 2000 compared to 43% in 1995. However, there are two groups of young people who are doing less well – boys and some minority ethnic groups. While 55% of girls achieve five or more higher grade GCSEs, only 44% of boys do so. And, while levels of attainment have increased for all ethnic groups, wide gaps in attainment remain, with especially low attainment among students of African Caribbean, Pakistani and Bangladeshi heritage (Owen et al, 2000; Cabinet Office, 2001b). For example, while 50% of students of white heritage obtain five or more GCSEs at grade A to C in year 11, only 37% of students of African Caribbean heritage, 30% of students of Pakistani heritage and 30% of students of Bangladeshi heritage do so. On the other hand 62% of students of Indian heritage and 70% of students of Chinese heritage do so.

As far as NVQ level 3 is concerned, currently 51% of young people reach this level at age 19 – a considerable increase from the 35% who did so in 1993. This increase is due to both the increasing proportion attaining 'A' level qualifications as well as the increasing proportion achieving vocational qualifications (mainly GNVQs) at NVQ level 3.

As far as *adult* attainment is concerned, currently 74% of the economically active adult population are qualified to NVQ level 2 or above and 51% of the economically active adult population (47% of the whole adult population of a working age) are qualified to NVQ level 3 or above. There has been considerable progress in relation to the latter in particular, over recent years. Only 36% of economically active adults were qualified to this level in 1993. At NVQ level 4 or equivalent the proportion of economically active adults who are qualified to this level has increased over the same period from 22% to 27%.

Inequalities in workforce qualifications

The qualifications held by different groups in the workforce vary considerably (see Table 2.1). Inequalities in educational attainment are apparent in relation to economic status, age, gender, ethnicity and occupation. From the table we can see that the following groups are the least likely to hold formal qualifications:

• the ILO unemployed (22% are without qualifications);
• the economically inactive (31% are without qualifications);
• individuals aged over 50 (21% are without qualifications);

Table 2.1: Qualifications of the workforce: highest NVQ equivalent qualification, England (2001)

	No qualification	NVQ 1	NVQ 2	NVQ 3	NVQ 4+
Economic status					
Economically active	11.7	14.3	22.8	24.5	26.8
In employment	11.1	14.0	22.6	24.7	27.4
ILO unemployed	21.8	19.0	25.5	19.8	13.9
Economically inactive	30.7	15.8	21.2	20.7	11.6
Age					
16-24	8.3	10.3	37.7	29.3	14.5
25-49	8.8	13.9	22.7	23.8	30.8
50+	21.1	17.9	13.6	23.4	24.0
Gender					
Male	10.9	14.1	18.1	29.9	26.9
Female	12.6	14.5	28.6	17.7	26.6
Ethnicity					
White	11.7	13.5	23.3	25.0	26.4
Non-white	11.6	24.4	15.6	17.4	31.1
Occupation					
Managers and administrators	6.9	9.6	20.2	26.2	37.0
Professional	0.6	3.8	4.1	8.7	82.8
Associate professional and technical	1.8	7.1	14.2	20.4	56.6
Clerical and secretarial	8.5	15.2	38.5	23.0	14.8
Craft and related	13.5	12.7	15.8	50.8	7.2
Personal and protective service	12.7	18.9	29.7	27.8	10.9
Sales	14.3	14.8	36.2	23.0	11.6
Plant and machine operatives	22.6	30.0	20.2	22.9	4.3
Other	33.2	23.0	24.5	15.5	3.7

Source: Labour Force Survey (2001, first quarter)

• individuals who are employed in manual occupations (up to 23% are without qualifications).

There are also inequalities in qualifications in terms of gender. The proportion of women without qualifications is only slightly above that for males but the proportion of women qualified to NVQ level 3 is considerably below that for men. The proportion of women who are qualified to NVQ 2, on the other hand, is considerably higher than for men. Women are clearly under-represented in education and training at level 3, experiencing only limited progression from level 2.

In terms of ethnic group a slightly higher proportion of people of white heritage than people of all other heritage are qualified to NVQ level 3 and above, though on the other hand, the proportion of the latter qualified to level 4 exceeds that among people of white heritage. However, this situation masks considerable differences across a range of ethnic groups. Individuals of Bangladeshi (24%), Pakistani (19%) and African Caribbean (16%) heritage are much less likely to hold any qualifications than those of white (12%), black African (8%) and Indian (10%) heritage. In relation to higher level qualifications, only 28% of people of Bangladeshi heritage and 39% of people of Pakistani heritage are qualified to NVQ level 3 or above compared to more than 50% of people of white heritage.

This issue is important, but not only in relation to issues of equal opportunity and social inclusion. Minority ethnic groups are a very rapidly growing component of the population, having grown by 21% between 1991-99 compared to an overall population growth of 1.2%. They are expected to account for more than half of the growth of the working age population over the next 10 years (Owen et al, 2000). Moreover, this growth will be even greater in localities with high minority ethnic populations, for example, London, Bradford, Leicester, and a number of smaller towns in the North West. The labour force growth is expected to be particularly strong among the black heritage and South Asian heritage communities.

One other feature of the distribution of workforce qualifications as set out in the table is worthy of note. Nearly 37% of managers are only qualified, at best, up to NVQ level 2. Indeed, only the same proportion is qualified to NVQ level 4 or above. This represents an important deficiency in the qualification levels of a significant proportion of contemporary managers.

A particularly important aspect of the inequalities in workforce skill levels is *basic skills*. It is estimated that approximately one in five adults (19%) has less literacy than is expected for an 11-year-old (that is, below or at entry level, but below NVQ level 1). Problems relating to numeracy are even more severe: approximately half (48%) of all adults have numeracy difficulties (again, skills below those expected of an 11-year-old), with 23% being classed as having 'very low' numeracy (Bynner and Parsons, 1997; Moser, 1999).

The Moser report estimates that there are around seven million adults who are 'functionally' illiterate or innumerate, but that only 250,000 are taking part in relevant study to overcome these problems. Moreover, around 500,000 people whose first language is not English, have little command of the English language. The issue is particularly prevalent among Punjabi and Bengali speakers. One in four of those whose first language is not English obtained a 'zero score' in the relevant test, meaning that they could not fill in their name and address (reported in Moser, 1999, p 19).

One way of putting the basic skills issue in context is to examine the results from the most recent international survey of literacy and numeracy. The International Adult Literacy Survey (OECD, 2000) identifies three different aspects of what they call literacy: *prose* (understanding information from texts, for example, newspapers, instruction manuals); *document* (using information from various formats including timetables, maps, tables, and charts); and *quantitative* (applying arithmetical operations to numbers used in printed materials). Table 2.2 summarises the main relevant results for the UK. In relation to each of the three aspects of literacy and numeracy, at least half of the individuals studied were found to have skills below level 3, the level identified by the OECD as "a suitable minimum for coping with the demands of everyday working life in a complex advanced society". This is clear evidence of a serious skill deficiency across the majority of the adult population. Furthermore, the proportion of adults at level 1 in the UK is the third highest of the 12 countries for which this information is provided by the OECD. Again, this represents a serious skill deficiency which is a key component of social exclusion for this significant minority − one in four adults − of the adult population.

The OECD make three telling conclusions: formal education is the main determinant of literacy proficiency in most countries, including the UK; there is a statistically significant correlation between people's literacy levels and their parent's length of time spent in education; and age and occupation are the major determinants of basic skills levels.

With regard to qualifications, there are significant differences between social groups in the extent to which people are disadvantaged in relation to basic skills development. The Adult Literacy in Britain Survey (1997) indicates that the following groups are among those most likely to have the lowest level of basic skills (see also Bynner and Parsons, 1997; Moser 1999):

- older people (aged over 45);
- those with low levels of educational attainment;

Table 2.2: Percentage of adults with poor literacy and numeracy skills, UK

	Level 1 skills (very poor) %	Level 2 skills (weak) %	Total levels 1 and 2 %
Prose	22	30	52
Document	23	27	50
Quantitative	23	28	51

Source: Coleman and Keep (2001)

- the unemployed and economically inactive;
- manual social groups;
- those with a low income;
- those from minority ethnic groups.

Participation in learning

Increased participation in education and training is a prerequisite to an increase in qualification levels and attainment. It is also a prerequisite to reducing skill inequalities. However an increase in participation will not necessarily result in a corresponding increase in measurable achievement, as a considerable proportion of learning that is undertaken is not accredited. While potentially contributing to skills acquisition in the workforce, increases in participation may make only a limited contribution to the acquisition of actual qualifications, even if they increase skill levels more generally. However, in a world where skills need to be increasingly portable (across occupations and sectors) their certification, as evidence to future employers, is of considerable importance. Moreover, of course, increasing participation needs to be paralleled by the successful completion of learning episodes so that learning outcomes are raised alongside participation improvements. We now examine, in turn, young peoples' participation, and then that of adults.

Young people's participation

The participation of young people in post compulsory education and training is largely governed by their destinations after completion of their GCSEs: destinations at age 16 provide us with a good indication of participation in post compulsory education. Figure 2.2 shows the destinations of school leavers in England in 1991 and 1999. It can be seen that the proportion of school leavers remaining in education has increased markedly – by around 10 percentage points – while, in parallel, there have been decreases in the proportion of school leavers entering both government supported training and employment, as well as in the proportion who are unemployed. This increase in 'staying on' rates, stimulated by a combination of factors including increasing levels of attainment pre 16 (in part following the replacement of 'O' levels with GCSEs), increasing choice of education related options post 16, and changing labour market conditions for young people, is an important factor that has contributed to the increase in attainment levels across the workforce as a whole (Coleman and Keep, 2001).

The growing proportion of young people remaining in post-compulsory education is evident from figures on the proportion of 16- to 19-year-olds engaged in full-time education and training. In 1992, 49% were participating in full-time education: by 2000, this had increased to 57%.

On the other hand, it should be noted that the participation rates of young people have not increased since 1997. Moreover, young people's participation in full-time education remains well below that of most other OECD countries

Figure 2.2: Destinations of school leavers in England (1991 and 2000)

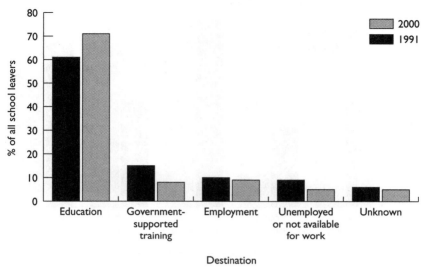

Source: DfES (2001)

(DfEE, 2000, table 7.5). The UK participation rate of 18-year-olds in full-time/part-time education (in programmes lasting a year or more) is 49% – a rate which is above only those in Turkey and Mexico. It is below the participation rate in all other 25 OECD countries including those in some of our main competitors: the US (63%); Ireland (71%); the Netherlands (78%); Belgium (80%); Germany (86%); and Sweden (96%).

Furthermore, the rapid growth in student numbers in higher education that took place primarily over the period 1988-94 has now levelled off. The percentage of 18- to 21-year-olds in higher education rose from around 15% in the 1980s to over 30% by 1994. It has barely increased since that time, with just 5% more full-time undergraduates in 2000-01 than in 1996-97 (HEFCE, 2001).

Adult participation

Figure 2.3 shows the proportion of adults that have participated in learning in the UK, as measured by a survey carried out by National Institute for Adult and Community Education the national organisation for adult learning, in both 1996 and 1999 (Sargant, 2000). The survey, of more than 5,000 adults aged 17+, indicates that only about 40% of adults have participated in learning at some point over the last three years. Moreover, levels of participation in learning have remained relatively constant since 1996 and some 37% of adults have not participated in learning since they completed their full-time education.

Overall levels of participation in learning are, of course, important in relation to the potential for future skills development. But the extent to which learning

Figure 2.3: Participation in learning among adults, UK (1996 and 1999)

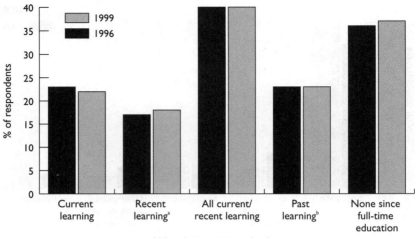

ª last 3 years
ᵇ more than 3 years ago

Source: Sargant (2000)

is undertaken by different groups in the population is also important. For example, Bynner (in Coffield, 2001, p 59) concludes that: "lifelong learning for all may be considered to have arrived when the differentials between the traditionally disadvantaged and advantaged groups, as defined by a range of social and economic variables, are eliminated or much reduced".

The scale of these differentials, and evidence that they are not being systematically reduced, is clearly demonstrated in the findings of the NIACE survey presented in Table 2.3. Considerable inequalities exist in participation, with the following groups among the least likely to have engaged in current or recent learning:

• older people – participation reduces significantly with age; for example 41% of those aged between 45-54 participate in learning compared to 70% of 20- to 24-year-olds;
• the economically inactive – 30% of those not working participate compared to 50% of those in jobs;
• skilled, semi-skilled and unskilled working class – an average of around 30% participate compared to 51% of the lower middle class;
• those who finished their initial full-time education at the earliest age – with less than 20% participating compared to 58% of those who completed their full-time education aged over 18.

It is also important to note that levels of participation across all groups have remained relatively constant over the period 1996–99, with the exception of large increases in participation (of around 7 to 8 percentage points) occurring among part-time employees and those not working.

The significant divide between 'learners' and 'non learners' is also apparent when considering the likelihood of participation in learning in the future. The NIACE survey found that 38% of all adults were either very or fairly likely to take up learning in the next three years. However, while this included 76% of those who are currently learning and 60% of those who have participated in learning in the past three years, only 25% of past learners and 12% of those who have undertaken no learning since leaving full-time education indicated that they are likely to participate in the future.

Table 2.3: Participation in education and training among different groups in the population

	% who had participated in current or recent (last 3 years) learning (1996)	% who had participated in current or recent (last 3 years) learning (1999)
All	40	40
Gender		
Male	43	41
Female	38	40
Age		
17-19	86	81
20-24	65	70
25-34	48	50
35-44	43	47
45-54	36	41
55-64	25	30
Employment status		
Full-time	49	51
Part-time	42	50
Unemployed	40	41
Not working	23	30
Retired	20	16
Socioeconomic class		
Upper middle and middle class	53	58
Lower middle class	52	51
Skilled working class	33	36
Semi- and unskilled working class	21	24
Terminal age of full-time education		
Under 16	20	19
16-17	39	42
18+	59	58

Source: Sargant (2000)

Barriers to achievement

So, overall participation rates have not increased in recent years among young people or among adults and there are substantial differences in participation rates across many social groups. What then are the main barriers to increasing participation and thereby to increasing the overall skills and qualifications of the workforce as well as to reducing existing inequalities in learning participation?

The National Advisory Centre for Education and Training Targets (NACETT) (2000) identify a number of barriers in their final assessment of progress towards the previous National Learning Targets, prior to their abolition and the passing of responsibility for the pursuit of national learning targets to the Learning and Skills Council established in 2001:

- relatively low achievement among boys, when compared to that of girls, at ages 11 and 16;
- large disparities in performance across LEAs in schools at all ages;
- vocational qualifications are not given the same parity of esteem as academic qualifications;
- insufficient numbers of the workforce are trained to level 3;
- the non-completion rate for vocational qualifications is high;
- young women are significantly under represented in education and training at level 3;
- adults face barriers such as lack of finance, lack of time and early unhappy learning experiences.

More generally, individuals who would be termed 'non-learners' can be split into two different groups (Hillage et al, 2000). Firstly, those individuals who would like to undertake learning but are unable to do so because of external barriers and, secondly, those who do not want to engage in learning, through lack of confidence and motivation, and disaffection.

In the NIACE survey respondents (with the exception of those who had stated that they are 'very likely' to learn in the future) were asked if anything was preventing them from learning. The key barriers identified included:

- not interested/don't want to – 27%
- work/other time pressures – 17%
- too old/ill/disabled – 15%
- childcare/caring responsibilities – 8%
- cost – 7%.

A major recent survey undertaken for the OECD (2000) (see Table 2.4) suggests that time and cost are the key barriers facing those who would like to participate in job-related training but who have not done so in the last year. The OECD benchmarks the situation in the UK with that in other OECD countries. In relation to the barriers to participation identified by those who have not participated in job-related training a relatively high proportion of those in the

Table 2.4: Perceived barriers to participation in job or career-related continuing education and training among employed adults (1994-95)

	% not taking job-related training in last year	% of those not taking training who wanted to participate	Situational barriers					Institutional barriers			Dispositional barriers	
			Too busy/ lack of time	Too busy at work	Family responsibilities	Lack of employer support	Course not offered	Too expensive/ no money	Lack of qualifications	Inconvenient time	Language	Health
Australia	59	24	52	14	6	5	6	18	2	6	2	1
Belgium	78	16	59	19	7	5	1	7	2	4	3	–
Canada	62	30	53	11	21	9	6	21	2	10	–	–
Ireland	76	15	40	21	11	4	12	24	3	7	–	–
Netherlands	65	24	54	17	6	10	5	13	1	6	–	3
New Zealand	49	26	65	66	28	9	10	25	4	38	1	2
Poland	83	13	43	19	17	11	14	25	1	6	1	5
Switzerland (French)	74	32	44	21	4	9	11	18	3	7	0	2
Switzerland (German)	65	27	48	21	6	13	18	11	1	7	2	1
United Kingdom	44	20	37	22	8	17	13	25	1	17	–	2
United States	53	18	53	24	13	7	3	30	–	7	1	2

% of non-participants in job-related training who gave various reasons for not taking job-related continuing education and training that they wanted to take

Source: OECD (2000, p 204, Table C.7.7)

UK identify cost, lack of employer support, time pressures at work, and other institutional barriers (including provision of courses and inconvenient time of courses) as barriers, as compared to their OECD counterparts. These are the issues that need to be addressed, in stimulating participation.

In order to raise participation it will be necessary, however, not only to remove barriers but also to encourage people to believe that it is desirable to engage in learning and skills acquisition. So, the converse to considering barriers to participation is to examine the factors that motivate individuals to learn. The importance of employment as a catalyst to participation in education and training is shown in the NIACE survey which found that 47% of those who had undertaken learning had done so for work related reasons: 35% had done so for personal development; and 11% had done so for reasons associated with education and progression.

Regional and local differences in qualifications and participation

Skill levels also vary considerably across different parts of the country (Campbell et al, 1999). In terms of regional variations in qualification levels, the proportion of those of working age who have attained NVQ level 3 varies by fully 10 percentage points – from highs of 47% in London and 46% in the South East to lows of 37% in the North East and 38% in the West Midlands. A similar pattern emerges in relation to the proportion of adults achieving level 4. London has 31% qualified to this level or above, compared to just 18% in the North East.

The variations in skill levels are, however, even more considerable across localities. The proportion of adults achieving NVQ level 3 varies by up to 22 percentage points – from highs of 54% in the central London Learning and Skills Council (LSC) area, 53% in Surrey and 51% in Avon; to 36% in South Yorkshire, 33% in Tees Valley and 32% in the West Midlands. At NVQ level 4 attainment rates vary by 26 percentage points, equivalent to more than the national average qualified to this level. Central London has the highest rate of 41% and Tees Valley has the lowest at 15%.

GCSE attainment rates tend to be highest in the south of England. The percentage of pupils achieving five or more GSCEs grade A–C is above the average for England in the South East, South West, and in eastern regions. The South East has the highest percentage of pupils achieving five or more GSCEs grades A–C at 54% while the North East has the lowest at 41% – a difference of 13 percentage points. In each region. It is worth noting that females outperform males by 10 or 11 percentage points.

It is a matter of particular concern that those localities which are 'skill poor' tend to be so in terms of schoolchildren and among the workforce of the area as a whole. Figure 2.4 presents the results of an analysis of the (around) 100 local education authorities for which comparable data exists for attainment at Key Stage 2 (age 11), GCSE (age 16) and the proportion of the local workforce who are without qualifications.

Figure 2.4: Spatial skill variations: relationships across levels of qualification

	% Key Stage 2	% attaining 5 GCEs	% workforce with no qualifications	% working population low numeracy
% attaining level 4 at Key Stage 2 (1998)		0.791**	0.663**	0.642**
% attaining 5 GCSE (A-C) (1998)	0.791**		0.598**	0.686**
% workforce with no qualifications (1997)	0.663**	0.598**		0.663**
% working population with low numeracy	0.642**	0.686**	0.663**	

Note: ** indicates significance at 0.01% level.
Source: Campbell (1999), page 10

There is a strong, clear systematic relationship across the four 'levels'. Localities with a poor performance at Key Stage 2 tend to have a poor performance at GCSE and also have a poorly qualified local workforce. This implies the existence of a structural weakness in local skill formation, development, and retention in some localities. On the other hand, localities which have a strong performance at Key Stage 2 tend to also perform well at GCSE and have a highly qualified workforce.

Connected to these substantial geographical variations in qualification attainment there are also major geographical variations in participation in learning. Not only do young people within the south generally outperform those in the north, they are also more likely to participate in full-time education. London, the South West and South East regions have above average participation rates of 16- to 19-year-olds in full-time education. Participation is highest in London where 67% of individuals aged 16-19 are in full-time education compared to the North East where only 54% participate in full-time education. However, the location of universities may bias these figures in favour of regions with large scale university provision.

If we examine variations in participation at the more local level of the 47 LSC areas, substantial variations are evident in young peoples' participation rates in full-time education. Gloucestershire has the highest proportion of individuals aged 16-19 participating in full-time education, at 76%, while Suffolk has the lowest at 47% – a difference of 29 percentage points. The three 'best performing' LSC areas are Gloucestershire (76%), Surrey (76%) and North Yorkshire (75%). In contrast, the three LSC areas with the weakest performance are Suffolk (47%), Shropshire (49%) and Humberside (50%).

Table 2.5 shows participation in learning for adults (individuals aged 17 or over) within each of the English regions in 1999. Here the disparity between regions is not as marked. As can be seen, participation in current or recent learning is highest in the East Midlands and East Anglia (48%) and lowest in the north and the West Midlands (34%), and the South West (37%). The table

Table 2.5 Participation in learning by Government Office Region

	Base – all respond	Current learning (%)	Recent learning (%)	All/ recent learning (%)	Past learning (%)	None since full-time ed (%)
London	603	26	20	46	18	36
South East	953	23	19	42	23	35
South West	418	23	15	37	23	40
East Anglia	183	27	20	48	25	27
East Midlands	359	27	21	48	18	34
West Midlands	456	16	18	34	26	40
North West	558	20	21	41	24	35
Yorkshire and Humberside	424	23	18	42	23	35
North	264	17	17	34	23	43
Total (UK)	5,054	22	18	40	23	37

Source: Sargant (2000)

also indicates that the proportion of individuals who have not participated in formal learning since leaving full-time compulsory education is above the UK average in the North (43%), West Midlands (40%) and the South West (40%).

Training

Training provision

Training is a major means through which the skills of the workforce can be enhanced. However, the distribution of job related training is highly unequal. Broadly speaking, the highest levels of formal workplace training are received by those in professional and associate professional/technical jobs; those who are already well-qualified; and younger workers (see Table 2.6). With respect to occupation, employees within professional (50%), associate professional/technical (42%), and managerial/administrative occupations (28%) are those most likely to receive training. Employees working in plant/machine operative (15%), craft (18%), and 'other' occupations (14%) are least likely to receive training. Moreover, this inequality in training participation is cumulative – those who do not receive it in one year tend also to be excluded in future years (Green, 1999).

An examination of job-related training by highest qualification shows that 43% of employees qualified to NVQ level 4 or above received training, compared to around 28% of those qualified to NVQ levels 2 and 3, and 20% of those qualified to NVQ level 1. Only 10% of those with no qualifications receive any formal workplace training.

It is also the case that older workers are less likely to receive job-related training than younger employees. Just over one fifth (21%) of employees aged 50 or above participate in formal job-related training compared to nearly one

Table 2.6: Percentage of employees receiving training[a]

	Winter 2000/01
Occupation	
Managers/administrators	27.6
Professional	50.3
Associate professional/technical	41.6
Clerical/secretarial	27.1
Craft and related	18.2
Personal/protective	34.1
Sales	25.2
Plant/machine operatives	14.5
Other	14.0
Full-time/part-time	
Full-time	30.4
Part-time	24.8
Permanent/temporary	
Permanent	30.6
Temporary	33.6
Qualifications	
No qualifications	9.9
NVQ 1	20.1
NVQ 2	28.4
NVQ 3	27.8
NVQ 4+	43.3
Age	
16-24	38.5
25-49	30.6
50+	20.6
All employees	28.9

[a] In the 13 weeks prior to the survey.

Source: Labour Force Survey (Winter, 2000/01)

third (31%) of those aged 25-49 and two fifths (38%) of those aged between 16 and 24.

Participation in training also varies by sector. The sectors with the highest proportions of employees who participate in training activity are: public administration, education and health (24% in the 13 weeks prior to being surveyed); banking, finance and insurance (17%); and the utilities (18%). The lowest proportions are in agriculture, forestry and fishing (8%); manufacturing and construction (12%); and transport (11%).

Establishment size is also an important factor in the level and type of workplace training provided (see Table 2.7). Smaller establishments are less likely to provide formal workplace training than larger ones, especially in respect to off-the-job training. One third of employers within the 1-4 employee size band, and more than half in the 5-24 size band, provide off-the-job training, compared to over three-quarters of establishments employing 25 or more employees. This disparity may reflect the greater difficulties that smaller establishments face in resourcing training, and arranging operational cover for workers undertaking off-the-job

Table 2.7: Provision of training by establishment size (2000, %)

No of employees	Off-the-job	On-the-job	Both
1-4	33	59	22
5-24	54	81	45
25-99	78	89	70
100-99	92	94	87
200-499	96	93	90
500+	98	92	90
Total	41	66	31

Source: Spilsbury (2001)

training. Smaller establishments are also less likely to have an internal training capacity, to be in a position to benefit from economies of scale through bulk buying of training, or to have a formal business and/or training plan. It has also been suggested that the lower incidence of workplace training in smaller establishments can be partly explained by the generally lower perceived need for training, infrequent recruitment, and/or limited changes in technology or working practices among their employees (Johnson, 1999).

Training quality

The quantity and distribution of workplace training is important but it is also necessary to consider the quality of training provided. Unfortunately, measuring the quality of training is difficult and it is necessary to rely on proxy indicators, such as whether or not training leads to a qualification, and the type and duration of training provided.

In terms of qualifications, 31% of job-related training leads to some sort of qualification (Labour Force Survey, 2000/01). Findings from the Learning and Training at Work 2000 survey (Spilsbury, 2001) indicate that 46% of employers who provide off-the-job training report that some of the training leads to formal qualifications.

The extent to which training leads to qualifications is more prevalent in larger organisations. They are much more likely to offer off-the-job training which leads to formal qualifications than are smaller organisations. Only 39% of businesses in the 1-4 size band and 51% in the 5-24 size band provide training leading to formal qualifications. This compares to 73% in the 100-99 size band and 90% in the 500+ size band.

The skills of the unemployed and the economically inactive

In order to access employment opportunities, those who are currently unemployed or economically inactive need to possess skills which are required on the labour market. The unemployed/economically inactive also represent a potential, but currently unused, source of labour availability. On both counts, if their skill base is inadequate, this poses problems simultaneously locking people out of access to jobs and potentially contributing to the existence of skill shortages in conditions of expanding employment.

The qualification levels and occupational background of the long-term unemployed and economically inactive are, in fact, markedly different from those of people currently in jobs, creating an 'imbalance' between the pattern of skills demand and available supply.

The most notable difference between those in employment, and those that are either long-term unemployed (as defined by ILO standards) or economically inactive, is that those in employment are much more likely to have higher level qualifications (NVQ level 3 and above), and individuals that are long-term unemployed or economically inactive are much more likely to have low level qualifications (NVQ levels 1 or 2), or no qualifications at all (see Figure 2.5).

Of the long-term unemployed, 29% and nearly 40% of the economically inactive, have no qualifications at all, compared to 13% of those in employment. Only 32% of the economically inactive and 27% of the long-term unemployed have NVQ level 3 equivalent (or above) qualifications, whereas 57% of the employed possess such qualifications.

Figure 2.6 sets out the previous occupation of the long-term unemployed and the economically inactive and compares it with the present occupation of those currently in work. It can be seen that the most obvious difference between the occupational structure of the employed and the occupational structure of the long-term unemployed and the economically inactive, is the substantially

Figure 2.5: Highest qualification level of those in employment, the long-term unemployed and the economically inactive, England (December 2000-February 2001)

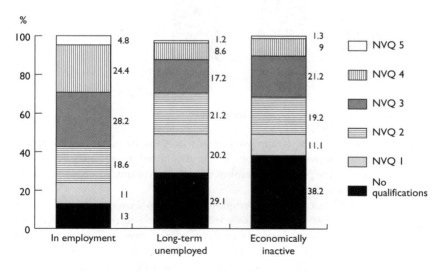

Source: Labour Force Survey (December 2000-February 2001)

Figure 2.6: Occupation of those in employment, and last occupation of the long-term unemployed and economically inactive, England (December 2000-February 2001)

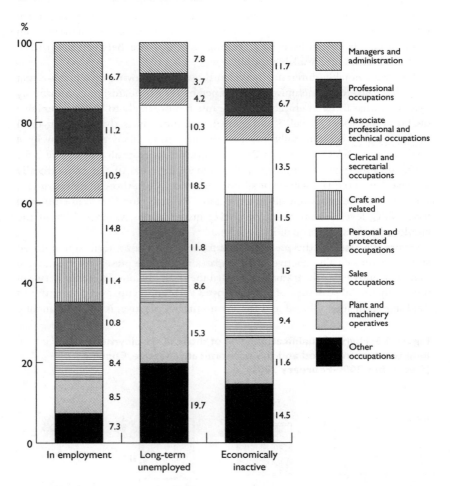

Source: Labour Force Survey (December 2000-February 2001)

smaller proportion of the latter two groups who were previously employed in managerial and professional roles. They also show a substantially higher proportion who were previously employed in craft and plant/machine operative occupations.

Around two fifths of those in employment are in managerial, professional and technical occupations, while only 16% of the long-term unemployed, and 24% of the inactive, were formerly in these occupations. Before they ceased being employed, 35% of the long-term unemployed and just over a quarter of the economically inactive were in non-craft-related manual occupations, but currently these occupations only account for 15% of employment. Just under a fifth of the long-term unemployed population was formerly employed in craft occupations while currently these occupations make up only 11% of employment.

We can conclude that there is clearly a very substantial skills deficit among the unemployed and economically inactive, which needs to be addressed if they are to effectively connect to evolving labour market opportunities. A failure to raise these skill levels will not only prejudice their ability to enter or re-enter the labour market on a sustainable basis but, in periods of high levels of employment, such a failure is likely to also constrain economic expansion if employers find it difficult to recruit.

Skill shortages

The weaknesses in the supply of skills that we have evidenced above may be expected to show up in the process of labour recruitment. Skill shortages will arise if employers are unable to recruit the workers they require because the skills they seek are not available in sufficient quantity. The existence of skill shortages is then an indicator of the inadequacy of existing overall skill levels in relation to current employer and labour market requirements.

In this section of the chapter we focus on the extent and nature of such skills shortages and how they vary by sector, occupation, and establishment size. The type of skills being sought by the employers who are experiencing skills shortages are also explored. The existence of skill shortages indicates the existence of a market failure, where skills supply is insufficient or inappropriate to the current needs of the labour market as articulated by employer requirements. Considerable evidence on such skill shortages is now available for England, thanks to major studies conducted by the Warwick Institute of Employment Research and IFF Ltd for the DfES (See Hogarth et al, 2001). Their research report is based on a large-scale survey of employers involving over 25,000 telephone interviews in late 2000 and early 2001.

It is important, however, to first make one general observation. The overall position on the balance of skills demand and supply may well tighten further over the coming years. It is anticipated (Wilson et al, 2001b) that over the period to 2010 in excess of two million additional jobs may be generated in Great Britain. In order to meet this increase in demand, activity rates will have to rise so as to increase the size of the labour force to levels that can sustain such jobs growth. An increase in activity rates from the current level of 78% to 81% would just about provide for the same overall quantitative balance between supply and demand as in 1999. It will be essential therefore to ensure that those entering the labour market over this period, including those moving into employment from the currently economically inactive, have the necessary skills required by employers in this context of continuing jobs growth. This is particularly critical in regions of rapid jobs growth. For example, in the South East and eastern regions, it is anticipated that labour demand is likely to rise faster than available supply (that is, new jobs are likely to grow faster than activity rates) by some 57,000 in the former case and 36,000 in the latter

(Wilson et al, 2001b), putting further pressure on the overall skills demand/ supply balance and necessitating further inflows of commuters and/or migrants.

In considering the issue of skill shortages it is important to distinguish between the terms *recruitment difficulties, hard to fill vacancies* and *skill shortage vacancies.* Recruitment difficulties occur in the external labour market where an employer identifies a vacancy as being hard-to-fill. Skill shortage vacancies are a sub-set of hard-to-fill vacancies and are characterised as a situation where at least one of the following reasons for the recruitment difficulties have been identified:

- low number of applicants with the required skills;
- lack of work experience that the company demands;
- lack of qualifications that the company demands.

We now go on to examine the overall level of skill shortage vacancies in the economy and the skills that are sought in these vacancies, before discussing their sectoral and occupational distributions and how they vary by establishment size.

The overall level of skill shortages

Around 14% of all employers reported vacancies at the time of the survey (see Table 2.8). This represents about 766,000 vacancies, just over half of which were described by employers as hard-to-fill, that is, 8% of all employers had a total of approximately 358,000 vacancies. Around half of these recruitment difficulties were skill related, so that 4% of all establishments experienced skill shortages, in total affecting 159,000 vacancies.

On the face of it, then, the overwhelming majority of establishments (96%) do not experience such skill shortage problems. However, as a proportion of those establishments who actually have vacancies, over one quarter (28%) experience skill shortages. Moreover, one fifth of all actual vacancies display a skill shortage and, as we shall see, the uneven duration, nature, and distribution of these skill shortages, by occupation, sector and location, means that they disproportionately affect some parts of the economy and labour market. It is also worth noting that skill shortages are very much a phenomena associated with small establishments. Those employing less than five people, account for 40% of all skill shortage vacancies and, indeed, the volume of these shortages are equivalent to nearly 30% of total employment in establishments of this size.

Table 2.9 shows the type of skills sought in connection with skill shortage vacancies. In addition to technical and IT related skills, there are significant levels of generic or transferable skills being sought. The most common skills sought are: 'other' technical and practical (34% of all skill shortage vacancies); advanced IT (20%); customer handling (16%); company specific (15%); communication (13%); and team working (11%).

Table 2.8: Overall number of vacancies, hard-to-fill vacancies and skill shortages (2001)

	% of all establishments reporting	Number of vacancies (000s)
All establishments		
All vacancies	14	766
Hard-to-fill vacancies	8	358
Skill-shortage vacancies	4	159
Establishments with 5 or more employees		
All vacancies	27	532
Hard-to-fill vacancies	14	232
Skill-shortage vacancies	6	94

Source: Hogarth et al (2001 pp 5 and 134, Tables 2.1 and 6.2)

The sectoral distribution of skill shortages

Skill shortage vacancies are disproportionately concentrated in five sectors of the economy: manufacturing; construction; wholesale and retail; business services; and health and social care. Together these sectors account for 79% of all skill shortage vacancies while employing 64% of the total workforce. As Table 2.10

Table 2.9: Skills sought in connection with skill shortage vacancies

Skill sought	% of all skill shortage vacancies
Basic computing	7
Advanced IT	20
Other technical/practical	34
Communication	13
Customer handling	16
Team working	11
Foreign language	2
Problem solving	8
Management	7
Numeracy	9
Literacy	7
Other	16
Company specific	15
Sales/marketing	1
Personal attributes	8
Experience	5
Driving	3

Source: Hogarth et al (2001, p 37, Table 2.19)

Table 2.10: Distribution of skill shortage vacancies by sector

	Distribution of total employment, England	Distribution of skill-shortage vacancies	Total number of skill shortage vacancies	Skill shortage vacancies as a % of employment	Skill shortage vacancies as a % of all vacancies
Agriculture	1	1	1,146	0.5	11
Manufacturing	17	13	21,443	0.6	28
Construction	4	10	15,438	1.7	39
Wholesale and retail	18	12	18,516	0.5	15
Hospitality	5	4	5,881	0.5	10
Transport and communications	6	5	7,215	0.6	14
Financial services	4	3	4,253	0.5	15
Business services	15	33	51,749	1.7	28
Public administration	6	2	2,729	0.2	10
Education	7	3	5,314	0.4	17
Health and social care	10	11	16,945	0.8	20
Other services	5	5	8,013	0.8	17
Total	100	100	159,081	0.8	21

Source: Hogarth et al (2001, pp 16 and 20, tables 2.7 and 2.9)

indicates, the proportion of skill shortage vacancies (column 2) is greater than the share of total employment (column 1) especially in construction and business services, but also in the health and social care sectors of the economy.

The occupational distribution of skill shortages

Table 2.11 indicates the distribution of skill shortage vacancies by occupation relative to the numbers employed in the different occupational groups, together with a 'density' measure of skill shortages. Skill shortage vacancies disproportionately occur in just three occupational groups, which account for well over half (56%) of skill shortages: professional; associate professional and technical occupations; and skilled trades occupations – yet these occupational groups only account for 30% of total employment. Skill shortage vacancies are least prevalent among managers and administrative/secretarial occupations.

One further aspect of skill shortages needs to be noted: their geographical distribution. Skill shortages are disproportionately concentrated in four regions, in terms of those regions experiencing a greater proportion of skill shortages than their share of employment. These are the eastern region, London, the South East and the South West. However, variations across the 47 LSC areas are substantially greater than those across regions. For example, 16% of establishments experience skill shortages in west Berkshire compared to just 1.3% in Northumberland (Green and Owen, 2001). Overall there is a broadly consistent relationship between the extent of skill shortages and areas which experience low unemployment and rapid employment growth.

Clearly actions designed to tackle skill shortages should reflect the sectoral,

Table 2.11: Distribution of skill shortage vacancies by occupation

	Distribution of total employment, England	Distribution of skill-shortage vacancies	Total number of skill shortage vacancies	Skill shortage vacancies as a % of employment
Managers/senior officials	16	5	7,436	0.2
Professional	13	18	28,886	1.1
Associate professional/technical	8	18	28,287	1.7
Administrative/secretarial	15	7	10,831	0.3
Skilled trades	9	20	31,592	1.7
Personal service	7	9	14,889	1.0
Sales/customer service	13	9	14,500	0.6
Process, plant, and machine operatives	11	9	14,440	0.7
Elementary occupations	8	5	8,100	0.5
Total	100	100	159,081	0.8

Source: Hogarth et al (2001, pp 14 and 26, tables 2.5 and 2.13a)

occupational and geographical distribution of such shortages. They should also focus on the nature of the skills sought and their deep concentration in micro establishments.

Skill gaps

Skill gaps are another measure of the inadequacy of the existing stock of skills available. They occur when there is a gap between the current skill levels of an organisation's workforce and those which are required to meet the organisation's objectives. They are, therefore, internal to organisations and represent a deficiency in the skills of the currently employed workforce. These gaps have been measured in the same studies conducted by the Warwick Institute for Employment Research (Hogarth et al, 2001).

Reported skill gaps

Skill gaps are measured in accordance with situations where establishments have a significant proportion of their workforce being reported as 'lacking proficiency'. More specifically, an internal skill gap is defined as existing where there is a lack of full proficiency (as perceived by employers), typically involving a third or more of the staff in at least one occupational area. We now consider these skill gaps and how they vary by sector, by occupation and establishment size.

Of all establishments 7% report the existence of such skill gaps and in total there may be around 670,000 employees who lack full proficiency in their job. Establishments suffering both skill shortages and skill gaps number 1%. Overall then, around 1 in 10 establishments suffer from a skill deficiency – either skill shortages or skill gaps, with almost twice as many establishments suffering from skill gaps as from skill shortages.

In relation to skill gaps the most sought after skill characteristics are: communication skills (40%); advanced/basic IT skills (33%); non–IT technical/ practical skills (32%); team working (32%); customer handling (30%); problem solving (26%); and management skills (22%).

The distribution of skill gaps varies by sector. The highest number of skill gaps (around 150,000 or 22% of the total number) are found in manufacturing establishments. The wholesale/retail and business services sectors account for a further 20% and 14% of skill gaps respectively. The lowest numbers of skill gaps are found in the agriculture, construction, education and financial services sectors. However, if we examine skill gaps as a proportion of employment in a sector they can be seen to disproportionately affect the hospitality sector (5.7% of total employment) and the manufacturing sector (4.8%), both of which are substantially above the average density (3.6% of total employment) of skill gaps. The education sector (1.4% of total employment), construction sector (2.8%), and health and social care sector (2.8%) have the lowest densities of skill gaps. In terms of the size of establishments in which they occur, skill gaps are greatest (as a proportion of employment) in the mid range of sizes of establishments, that is, those employing between 25 and 999 people. They are least in micro establishments employing less than five people, a situation which is the absolute converse of the pattern of skill shortages.

In terms of their occupational distribution the greatest concentrations of skill gaps are in the production and process operatives occupations (16%); sales (15%); and managers and administrative/secretarial; and 'other manual' occupations – (13%) in each case. Given the importance of managerial skill gaps, both in themselves, and in their indirect relationship with many other skill gaps (because of the key role of managers in decision making), it is worth noting that UK management skills are not always assessed highly by international standards (Bosworth, 1999; Johnson and Winterton, 1999; DTI, 2000).

The International Institute for Management Development provide comparative evidence across the G7 countries of business executives perceptions of management quality. The UK ranks fifth out of seven, behind Germany, the US, Canada and France. Johnson and Winterton (1999) conclude that UK managers are inadequately qualified compared to international competitors, a situation compounded by relatively poor levels of training and development. Bosworth (1999) found that UK managers are perceived to be poorer than their US and Japanese counterparts in every type of skill, especially in terms of their adaptability, entrepreneurial and technical skills; a situation which was more acute in smaller businesses. The best UK managers are comparable to the best in other countries, but there is a 'long tail' where the standard is significantly poorer.

The *occupational* pattern of skill gaps varies across establishments of different size with both the smallest establishments and the very largest having a substantial skill gap in relation to administrative/secretarial occupations. Skill gaps are also significant in respect of operatives in larger establishments and in respect of sales/customer service occupations in smaller establishments.

In terms of *sector*, almost half of all skill gaps in manufacturing are related to production and process operative occupations. Two fifths (40%) of skill gaps within the financial services sector are within administrative/secretarial occupations and just over one quarter (26%) are in sales and customer service occupations. Over one third (35%) of public administration sector skill gaps are in administrative/secretarial occupations and similarly over one third (37%) of health and social care skill gaps are in personal service occupations.

Finally, we should note that there are regional variations in skill gaps with the highest density (the size of the skill gap as a percentage of employment) being in the South West, followed by the East and West Midlands, and the South East (Hogarth et al, 2001, p 61). Variations at the level of the 47 LSCs are also substantial, with the proportion of establishments reporting skill gaps varying from a high of 25% or more in, for example, Cambridgeshire, West London and Bedfordshire to less than half of this level (12%) in Shropshire (Green and Owen, 2001).

Latent skill gaps

The evidence presented so far examines skill shortages and skill gaps as identified and reported by employers and management. However, some skill gaps may not be recognised by management and, moreover, some gaps will not appear until an organisation tries to improve its position in terms of product and process innovation, growth, or market position.

If an 'average' organisation were to 'raise its game' and begin to perform in line with the 'best' in their sector, this could reveal new skill gaps. 'Poorly performing' establishments which improved to become average would also experience gaps as they sought to improve. Moves to higher value added production/services, expansion into new markets, or shifts in their technological or organisational orientation, could uncover additional skill requirements that were necessary to enable organisations to achieve these changes and subsequent improvements in organisational performance, yet which were not currently met by their existing workforce.

Such latent skills gaps have three main dimensions. First, the skill needs of 'high performance' organisations exceed the sector average/norm, so that average or poorly performing organisations that improve their performance, will require higher levels of skills. Second, the skill gaps actually perceived by high performance organisations also exceed the sector average, so once average organisations become high performance organisations, they recognise the need for even higher skill levels. Third, a range of skills are required in order to move from an organisations existing situation to a high performance position, that is, there are 'transitional' skill requirements. We can think of the sum of these three elements as the scale of any latent skill gap.

A skill gap in the existing workforce may actually inhibit establishments from moving in this direction and achieving improved performance. Hogarth et al (2001) report that a substantial proportion of establishments indicate that they would wish to improve product or service quality but are constrained from doing so by the skills currently available in their existing workforce.

Such latent skill gaps constrain the potential for improved organisational performance and economic growth and are therefore of considerable importance. Their existence would also provide evidence of the existence of a 'low skill equilibrium' (on which see Chapter Five). This is a situation where organisations do not demand the skills that are actually required to achieve enhanced organisational success. In practice, such latent skill gaps are difficult to measure, but a range of studies based on the WIER/IFF employer survey, suggest the following (Hogarth and Wilson, 2001; Bosworth et al, 2001):

• Enterprises that adopt new working practices rather than cost reduction goals are much more likely to report higher levels of proficiency among their workforce. By implication, an enterprise that switched from a cost saving to a productivity goal is likely to downgrade its assessment of the proficiency of their current workforce.
• Those employers who adopt new technologies or new products are likely to be significantly less satisfied with the quality of their employees.
• There is a positive relationship between the existence of high-level, enterprise-wide goals and those establishments making human resource investments.
• Enterprises which exhibit consistently greater emphasis on product development also made higher investments in human resource development.
• The introduction of new technologies is positively linked to human resource investments.
• Cost-oriented enterprises are significantly less likely to advertise vacancies than the average and there was some evidence that they are less likely to report hard-to-fill vacancies. On the other hand profit-oriented enterprises are more likely to advertise vacancies and significantly more likely to report hard-to-fill vacancies.
• Larger enterprises and, in particular, those with more than one manager, are much more likely to recognise problems of worker proficiency.

Some empirical estimates of the possible scale of such latent skill gaps are contained in Bosworth et al (2001). If establishments who do not currently set explicit sales, cost, productivity or profits goals 'changed' so that their goals reflected those of just the 'average' establishment then:

• The incidence of internal skill gaps would rise by around 2.5 percentage points: an increase of around 10%.
• The incidence of skill shortage vacancies would increase by around 4.2 percentage points: an increase of almost one third.

The existence of such latent skill gaps demonstrate the importance of recognising that employer skill requirements are 'driven' by their business strategies. The 'product strategies' which companies pursue structure their demand for skills.

Certain strategies may lead to a pattern of workforce skill requirements which are largely appropriate to their current needs but which nonetheless do not provide the basis for long term enhanced competitiveness or performance through adaptation to changes in technology or the market place National Skills Task Force (NSTF) (2001a). Latent skill gaps are therefore gaps that need to be filled, if the UK is to continue its development as a high skill, high value added economy.

International comparisons

While skill levels have improved considerably over recent years it would be a serious mistake to conclude that this amounts to a successful outcome. Improvements need to be seen in international context as other counties similarly improve their skill levels over time. In fact the UK is not, overall, in a particularly strong position relative to many of our competitors and is quite possibly 'falling behind' over time as we shall see.

The gap between the UK's and other countries' skill levels appears to be greater among younger people than among older people (OECD, 2001b). The proportion of adults (those aged 25-64) who are qualified to upper secondary level education in the UK (defined broadly as NVQ level 2 or equivalent in the UK) is 62% – exactly equal to the OECD average. However, among older workers (aged 55-64) the UK is above the OECD average at 53%, compared to 45%. On the other hand, among younger workers (aged 25-34) the proportion qualified to upper secondary level education is 66% – fully 6% points behind the OECD average. In some OECD countries such as Japan, Korea, Norway and the Czech Republic, more than 90% of 25- to 34-year-olds have completed upper secondary level education.

A comparison of qualifications at NVQ levels 2 and above and 3 and above, between the UK, France and Germany does show some improvement in relative terms over the period 1994-98 (see Figure 2.7). Overall, however, the proportion of the workforce holding these levels of qualifications in the UK remains well below that in France and Germany. The only exception relates to NVQ level 3 and above, where, relative to France, the proportion in the UK is broadly similar. The gap at NVQ levels 2 and 3 is particularly large among 25- to 28-year-olds and the gap in vocational qualifications is larger still.

We now examine, in turn, international comparisons in performance at upper secondary education and tertiary education levels before turning to comparisons of participation in job related education and training.

Upper secondary education

How does the UK compare to other OECD countries on this broad indicator in relation to the proportion of young people (25- to 29-year-olds) and older people (50- to 54-year-olds) attaining upper secondary level education qualifications?

Survey data for 1998 (OECD, 2001b), presented in Figure 2.8 overleaf, shows

Figure 2.7: Qualifications at NVQ level 2+, 3+ or equivalent in the UK, France and Germany

(a) Qualifications at NVQ level 2+ or equivalent in UK, France and Germany (1998)

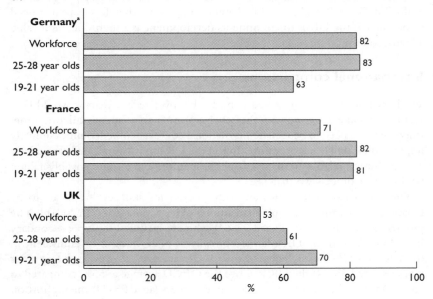

(b) Qualifications at NVQ level 3+ or equivalent in UK, France and Germany (1998)

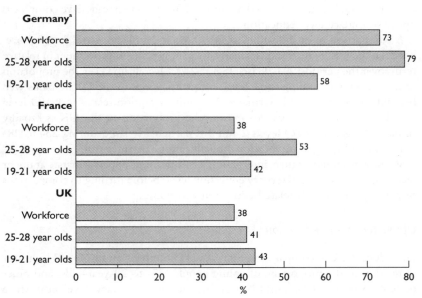

ª Germany data is 1997
Source: Steedman in DTI (2001)

that 64% of 25- to 29-year-olds in the UK have completed upper secondary level education, compared to an OECD average of 72%. This ranks the UK 19th out of 26 OECD countries – ahead of Turkey, Mexico, Portugal, Iceland, Spain, Italy and Poland, but behind all others. This position behind such major competitors as the US, Belgium, the Netherlands and Ireland, is a cause for serious concern. It is all the more so, as the measure used in the UK for these comparisons is NVQ level 2 or equivalent, which is relatively low when it is considered, for example, that the French measure of completion of upper secondary level education includes Baccalaureate qualifications.

In the case of older people, 54% of 50- to 54-year-olds have completed upper secondary education compared to an OECD average of 53% – thus ranking the UK 13th out of the 26 OECD countries. Comparing the situation of younger and older people we can therefore see that there has been a substantial improvement in upper secondary level education completion over the 20-30 years since the latter group left school (from 54% to 64%). However, in comparative terms:

- The improvement is less than for any other OECD country except one – Iceland.
- The ranking for young people's performance is worse in relative terms than for older people (19th compared to 13th).

The situation is therefore, in relative terms, deteriorating.

Tertiary education

Figure 2.9 compares the UK with other OECD countries in respect of the proportion of the same two age groups qualified to tertiary level.

In the case of both age groups the UK is just above the OECD average, being ranked 17th out of 26 in terms of the proportion of 30- to 34-year-olds who have attained tertiary level qualifications and 12th out of 26 in terms of the proportion of 50- to 54-year-olds who have done so.

In absolute terms there is considerable progress in the UK; from a position where 21% of 50- to 54-year-olds hold tertiary qualifications to one where 25% of 30- to 34-year-olds do so. However, in terms of international comparisons it is important to recognise that:

- the improvement in the UK is less than for most of the countries whose attainment rate for 50- to 54-year-olds is already higher than that for the UK, thus leading to a further widening of the gap;
- the international ranking of younger people's performance is worse than for older people.

Significantly, however, the UK has experienced a very substantial rise in enrolments in tertiary level education in the 1990s, a development which will feed through into the above position in future years with a considerable positive

Figure 2.8: Percentages of 25- to 29-year-olds and 50- to 54-year-olds who have completed upper secondary education

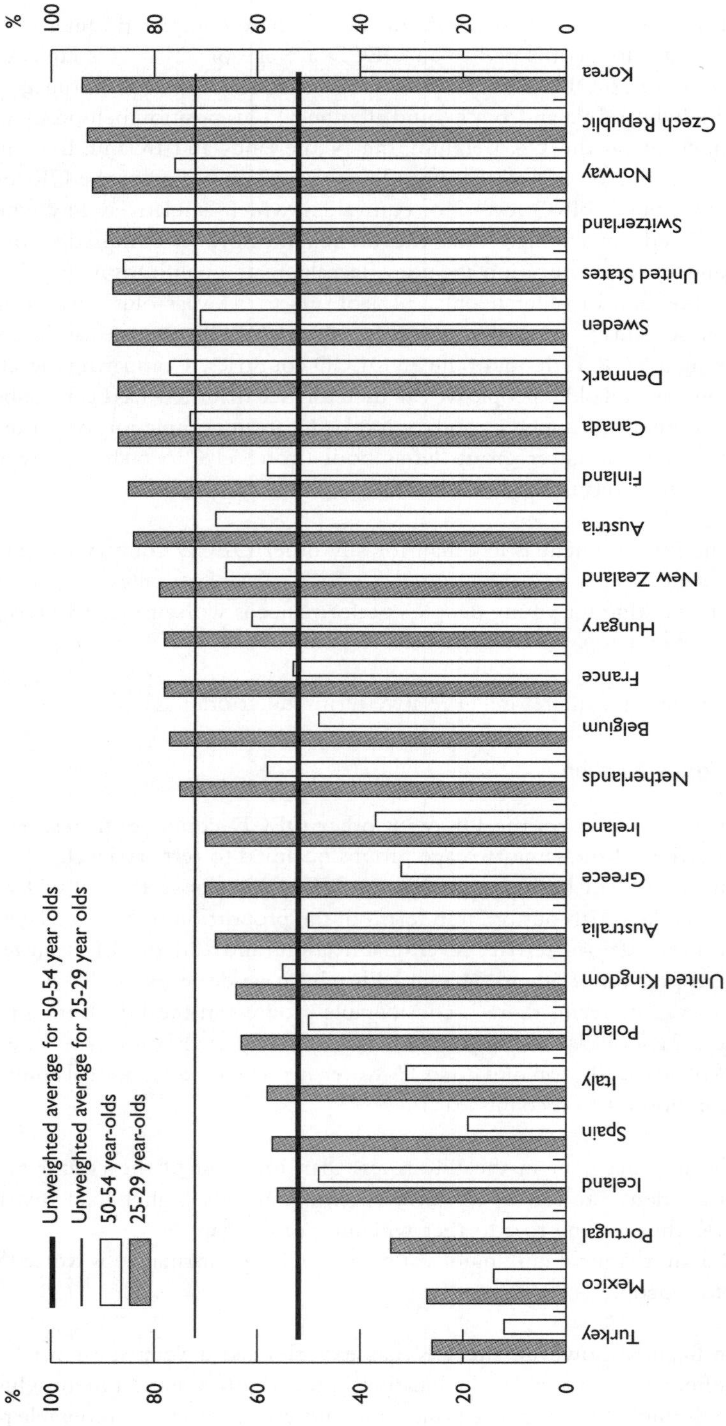

Legend:
— Unweighted average for 50-54 year olds
— Unweighted average for 25-29 year olds
□ 50-54 year-olds
▨ 25-29 year-olds

Countries (top to bottom): Korea, Czech Republic, Norway, Switzerland, United States, Sweden, Denmark, Canada, Finland, Austria, New Zealand, Hungary, France, Belgium, Netherlands, Ireland, Greece, Australia, United Kingdom, Poland, Italy, Spain, Iceland, Portugal, Mexico, Turkey

Source: OECD (2001b, p 48, Figure 2.2)

Figure 2.9: Proportions qualified at tertiary level across the OECD

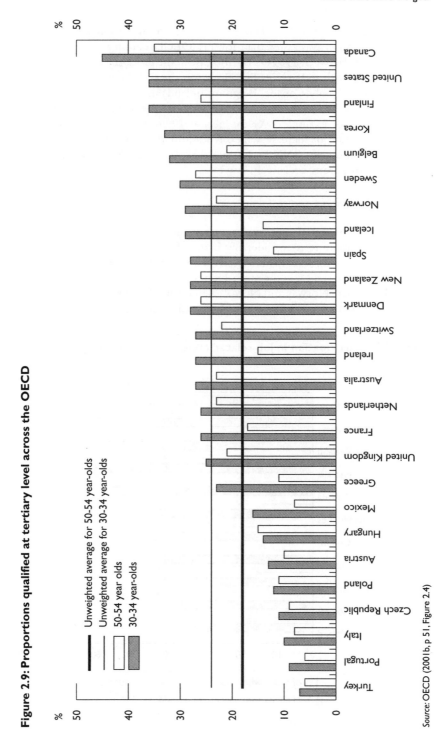

Legend:
- ▬ Unweighted average for 50-54 year-olds
- │ Unweighted average for 30-34 year-olds
- ☐ 50-54 year olds
- ▨ 30-34 year-olds

Source: OECD (2001b, p 51, Figure 2.4)

impact. Indeed, between 1990 and 1997 the growth in enrolments in the UK (at more than 50%) was faster than for any OECD country except Portugal (OECD, 2000). Between 1989-96 the increase in the proportion of the working age population with tertiary qualifications was the fifth highest of 19 OECD countries; behind only Canada, Belgium, Ireland, and Spain (OECD, 2001a, p 162, Chart C4.2). However, the UK growth rate has slowed in the later part of the 1990s. For example, over the period 1995-99 the growth slowed to around 20%, a rate of increase which is less, for the same period, than nine other OECD countries (OECD, 2001a, p 152, Chart C3.3) although most of these are starting from a relatively low base.

Continuing education and training

The UK's international comparative position with regard to continuing education and training is considerably better than it is with regard to upper secondary and tertiary level qualifications. The overall participation rate among those aged 16-65 is 44% – the sixth highest in the OECD, behind Finland, Denmark, Sweden, Norway and New Zealand (OECD, 2000, p 56, Figure 2.6).

Participation in job related continuing education and training is high, relative

Figure 2.10: Participation in job-related education and training

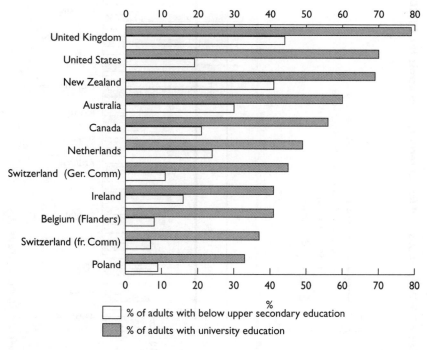

Source: OECD (2001b, p 91, Figure 3.7)

to other OECD countries. Of the 10 countries for which comparable data are available, the UK has by far the highest participation rate – 56% of employed adults had participated over the previous year compared to an OECD average of 34% (OECD, 2000, p 201, Table C.71). On the other hand, the average number of actual hours of training that each person undertook was the second lowest. O'Connell (1999) has shown that the total training 'effort', or 'volume', as measured by the combination of both these indicators (that is, the average duration in hours per employee) still puts the UK second only to New Zealand among OECD countries and on a similar level to the Netherlands and Ireland.

Training tends generally to reinforce already existing differences in skill attainment (OECD, 2000, p 202; OECD, 2001, p 90). Both the participation rate and mean number of hours of training per person vary by level of educational attainment, not only in the UK, but throughout the OECD countries. For example, even after controlling for employment status, company size and occupational groups, UK workers who make use of their literacy skills at work are 6 to 8 times more likely to receive support from their employers for training than those who use workplace literacy skills the least (OECD and Statistics Canada, 2000).

In the UK this process of exacerbating existing skill inequalities, while serious, is less severe than in most OECD countries (see Figure 2.10). The percentage of adults with below upper secondary level education who participate in job-related education and training is well below that for those with a University education in the UK (44% compared to 70%). However, both these figures are the highest in the 11 OECD countries studied. Moreover, for every workforce age group, UK participation in job-related education and training is above the OECD average (OECD, 2001b, p 144, Figure 1.1). However, this may be associated with relatively high labour turnover in the UK compared to many countries, and a consequently greater need for induction training; or it may be associated with a need to undertake 'remedial' training that is required because of the relatively low levels of skills in the workforce.

The International Adult Literacy Survey study (OECD and Statistics Canada, 2000) also report the relatively high levels of participation in job related education and training in the UK for those at relatively low literacy levels. The UK is ranked fourth in terms of participation for those with literacy levels 3/4/5 and sixth for those with levels 1 and 2 – although of course, the participation rates still vary enormously across the levels (22% at level 1, 34% at level 2, 54% at level 3 and 71% at level 4/5).

Adult literacy and numeracy

How does the UK fare in terms of international comparisons of literacy and numeracy proficiency? The IALS final report (OECD and Statistics Canada, 2000) provides a comprehensive assessment of a large-scale literacy study covering 23 countries over the period 1994-98. Literacy here covers a multiplicity of skills (for details see OECD and Statistics Canada (2000), Annex A) but generally the measurement of adult skills is measured in respect of three dimensions: prose (texts); document (in different formats); and, quantitative (number). In each case ability is expressed as a score – being defined as the point where a person has an 80% chance of successful performance from among the tasks included in the assessment. From the scores, five levels of literacy are identified:

- level 1 – very poor skills;
- level 2 – ability to deal only with simple tasks ;
- level 3 – a suitable minimum for coping with demands of everyday life and work in an advanced society. Roughly equivalent to the skill level required for successful secondary school completion and college entry;
- levels 4/5 – demonstrable command of higher order information processing skills.

In terms of the mean (average) level of literacy in society the UK ranks, out of 22 OECD countries:

- 13th on the prose domain
- 16th on the document domain
- 17th on the quantitative domain.

(OECD and Statistics Canada, 2000, pp 19ff, Figure 2.3)

Only five of the 23 countries (Hungary, Slovenia, Poland, Portugal and Chile) have a statistically significant lower mean proficiency on prose; six have a lower mean score on document literacy (Ireland, Hungary, Slovenia, Poland, Portugal and Chile); and four have a lower mean score on the quantitative scale (Slovenia, Poland, Portugal and Chile). These results demonstrate the existence of a very weak international position in terms of literacy and numeracy.

The study also demonstrates the high degree of skills inequality in the UK relative to many other countries. Fourteen of the countries (including the UK) have at least 15% of 16- to 25-year-olds performing at only literacy level 1. The UK figure is 22% or 23% depending on whether we are referring to the prose, document or quantitative domains. On average this is the sixth worst performance in terms of the proportion performing at this level. On the other hand the UK has a relatively high proportion scoring at level 5. This is clear evidence of a strong 'polarisation' of skill levels, a polarisation which is greater than in most other countries.

The key factors which are associated with proficiency in literacy and numeracy include:

- educational level – however, this does not guarantee the relevant literacy level, nor is it a necessary condition for it. For example, in the UK, 35% of those who have not completed upper secondary level education scored at level 3 or above, whereas in Sweden, 60% did so;
- first versus additional language – comparing the percentage at level 1 literacy between first and additional language speakers, the proportions are 22% and 54% respectively (p 160, Table 3.18);

- occupation – people's work experience and job position. For example, the occupational category in which the UK has, comparatively, the worst position in terms of the proportion of people at literacy level 3 or above, is craft/machine workers. At just 38% this is lower than in all 14 countries that were compared this way in the study – except for the US and Canada;
- labour force participation, and participation in voluntary activities – whether people are in employment and/or participate in voluntary work.
  (OECD and Statistics Canada (2000, p 165, Table 3.21)

Conclusions

The current 'skills position' as evidenced by the level, structure and composition of the supply of skills can be characterised as follows. It is important to recognise that substantial progress has been made in recent years in respect of increasing the country's skill levels. However, despite such progress, skill levels are not especially high in relation to those of many of our main competitor countries. The 'absolute' progress that has been made over time looks less positive when viewed against the progress of many other OECD countries. Furthermore, skills are unequally distributed across a range of social groups and, given the importance of the possession of skills to labour market success, this poses a serious threat to the process of social inclusion. The considerable inequalities in educational attainment; the existence of poor basic skills among a significant minority of the workforce; and the uneven and relatively low levels of participation in lifelong learning, all militate against increased social cohesion. Additionally they are also a barrier to enhanced competitiveness and, ultimately, to higher living standards as they restrict not only people's opportunities and life chances but the productivity and growth prospects of companies. The existence of skill shortages and the occurrence of skill gaps are indicators of a 'skills deficient' economy.

Moreover, the existence of considerable regional and local differences in skill levels, and participation rates in lifelong learning, restrict the development of many parts of the country. They contribute to regional and local inequalities, an uneven pattern of economic development and restrict the smooth functioning of the overall economy through geographic disparities in labour market conditions in terms of both employment and skills.

The skills we currently have available are seriously deficient, therefore, in a number of respects. If we wish to build a future based on the development of a knowledge based economy; if we are to adapt effectively to changes in technology, to the pattern of consumer demand and to the ever shifting pattern of competitive advantage between countries, we will need to raise our skill levels significantly.

THREE

What skills do we need?

"The future belongs to those who prepare for it today." (Malcolm X)

Introduction

This chapter examines the extent and nature of recent, and projected future, skill needs in the UK. The ongoing process of economic change drives developments in the labour market and consequent skill needs. Changes in economic structure, consequent upon changes in the level and pattern of consumer demand; developments in technology (in both processes and products); changes in the organisational structure of companies and other organisations; and the shifting pattern of national competitive advantage, all contribute to shifting the level and structure of occupations, qualifications and other skills required in the UK labour market.

It is crucial to understand the nature of the changes in skills demand being provoked by evolving skill needs so that the pattern of skills supply can be adapted, if necessary, by public policy to match the changing requirements of the labour market. Unless skills supply successfully adapts to the changes in the nature of labour and skills demanded, a range of inefficiencies, imbalances and inequalities will arise including structural unemployment, skill shortages, skill gaps and redundant skills. Moreover, economic performance will be constrained, inflationary pressures potentially provoked and the economy will operate at a lower level of capacity and growth than would otherwise be the case.

This chapter outlines the main drivers, or determinants, of change in skill needs, before examining recent developments in the sectoral, occupational and qualifications structure of employment. It then goes on to examine likely future changes in occupational and qualifications requirements including the main contours of regional variations in skills demand. It also draws attention to the importance of 'replacing' the skills lost through retirement and occupational mobility, and to the increasing importance attached to generic skills.

The drivers of change

There are four main drivers of change (see Figure 3.1) which are combining to increase the potential importance of skills to people, organisations, and the economy (see, for example, Thurow, 1999).

Figure 3.1: The drivers of change

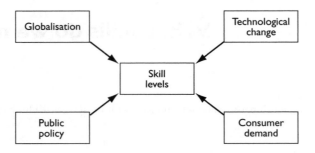

The process of *globalisation* is increasingly opening up local and regional economies and integrating them into the national economy, at the same time as the national economy is being integrated into the international economy. This integration takes the form of increasing connections and interdependency through: increased international trade (and inter-regional and inter-locality trade); increased international capital movements, including foreign direct investment (which also increases regional and local integration); and increased inter-firm collaboration in technology and product development. The development of global brands is one important aspect of this process. This increases both competitive pressures and opportunities, by progressively eliminating barriers to competition and widening the sphere within which market competition takes place. This then increases market opportunities but penalises those unable to compete effectively on this wider playing field. It makes it exceptionally difficult for relatively high wage economies to compete on costs and prices and has consequently engineered an increasing shift to higher value added, higher productivity goods and services; that have high information, knowledge, creativity and/or innovation components that are less easily replicated in lower wage economies.

This process of globalisation increasingly homogenises the availability of factors of production over time, leaving the skills and capacities of a nation's (or regions' or localities') people as the key differentiating factor in competitiveness (Reich 1993, 1999). It therefore forces adaptation to changing market conditions and increases the importance of skills as a differentiating feature in competitive markets, especially if an area or nation is moving up the 'value added' chain in order to compete effectively. The scale of this process of globalisation is indicated by the increasing ratio of trade to GDP in the OECD countries, which has increased from 13% to 21% between 1970 and 1997 and by the doubling of inward investment as a proportion of GDP over the same period (OECD, 2000).

The process of *technological change* and, in particular the integration, and rapid and widespread use, of information and communication technologies heightens competition through effectively 'collapsing' time and space. It also transforms competitive advantage, speeds up the process of economic change, and changes the organisation of work. Computer processing power doubles every 18 months. It has led to the development of an enormous range of new processes and products, including the internet, e-commerce and other advanced forms of telecommunication, as well as the development of bio-technologies. Some talk of the 'new economy'. Certainly the share of information and communications technology (ICT) sectors in UK GDP (defined as the office and computing equipment, radio, TV and communication equipment, and services sectors) has increased by 36% in the 1990s, to now account for nearly 7% of GDP.

The combination of globalisation and technological change is increasing skill requirements as work organisation and the nature of competitive advantage becomes more complex. The source of competitive edge in products and in processes becomes increasingly information and knowledge content. There are two major causes of the overall increase in skill requirements – and the associated deterioration of the situation facing unskilled workers: the expansion of trade with developing economies (Wood, 1995) and the continuous process of technological change (Machin and Van Reenan, 1998 and Berman et al, 1998). Wood argues that trade has lowered the economy wide relative demand for unskilled labour by around 20% in the advanced economies. Machin and Van Reenan argue that technological change is 'skill biased', favouring the employment and earnings of the more highly skilled, and simultaneously damaging the employment and earnings of the less skilled. Analysis of technological change in the UK and six other OECD countries shows that it is indeed associated with skill upgrading in all seven countries and, in particular, Berman, Bound and Machin find that changes within, rather than between, sectors are of most significance. Thus it is unlikely that product demand shifts induced by trade can be the key driver, as this would largely show up in shifts in skills and earnings between sectors. Indeed, they suggest that the technological change effect may be around eight times that attributable to increased trade. Moreover, the proportion of skilled workers in different sectors has increased, as have their relative earnings. It will be important, in the future, to update these studies (which relate largely to the 1980s) and to widen their focus from manufacturing to services. Nonetheless, technology and trade are clearly driving up the demand for higher level skills and driving down the demand for lower level skills.

Furthermore, the changing pattern of *consumer demand* in itself, at least in the more 'advanced' economies, is moving from relatively low value added, standard, materially heavy goods to high value added, higher quality, niche/bespoke market, light and 'stylish' goods and services (Coyle, 1999, Leadbetter, 2000). The income elasticity of demand for different products and services, together with changes in people's tastes and preferences generate an increasingly 'differentiated' pattern of production, with major ongoing restructuring of production to meet these needs. These are often 'knowledge rich' products and services, or ones which contain a high 'relational' content, where expertise as well as customer care, personal attention and face-to-face human interaction is important to organisational and personal success (for example, leisure, hospitality, travel, personal care), thus raising the role and value of generic skills.

Finally, *public policy*, at least in the advanced economies, is helping to drive up skill levels. Governments, recognising the changing nature of the economy and of competitive advantage, are shifting a whole range of policies towards the pursuit of higher levels of skill. Examples of this include: the target of increasing the proportion of young people who go to university to 50% of the cohort; the pursuit of a raft of policies on lifelong learning; and the major increases in education spending. But more generally, policy is supporting the rapid innovation and diffusion of technology and the process of globalisation – forces that will further drive up skills demand. The clearest aspect of this is the continuing development of the European Union – the process of establishing free internal trade, the free flow of capital and now a single monetary policy, currency and exchange rate, are designed, in part, precisely to strengthen and deepen the process of economic integration in Europe.

All these forces are driving up the demand for skills and making knowledge and 'investment in people' a core determinant of economic success – for companies, people, communities and nations.

On the other hand, for those without the required skills, and those not in demand in the knowledge rich economy and labour market, the situation is bleak. They face a world in which there are relatively few jobs which are appropriate to their skills compared to the past; low (or no) earnings growth, and an increasing gap between the overall economic condition of society and their own.

Overall trends in employment

During the 1990s there was an increase of just over one-and-a-half million in the total number of people employed in the United Kingdom. This growth reflects the recovery from a recessionary period of the early 1990s and also a structural 'long boom' of economic expansion over the period 1993 to date. Levels of employment are, at the time of writing in 2001, at a historical high, with unemployment levels lower than at any time since 1973. This growth in employment suggests an overall increase in the demand for skills by employers. At the same time however the *pattern* of demand in terms of skills required by employers has changed dramatically. What types of skills are in demand, and what skills are experiencing declining demand?

Sectoral trends

In this section of the chapter we review the main changes in the sectoral composition of employment that have taken place over the last decade and consider the main changes that are likely to occur over the next decade.

Changes in the sectoral composition of employment have important consequences for the kind of skills that are likely to be required. As the structure of goods and services produced changes, so do the jobs involved in producing these goods and services. In turn, the skills required by these jobs also change. Over the last decade, between 1991 and 1999, the sectoral pattern of jobs

Figure 3.2: Sectoral structure of UK employment (1991 and 1999) (numbers employed, 000s and %)

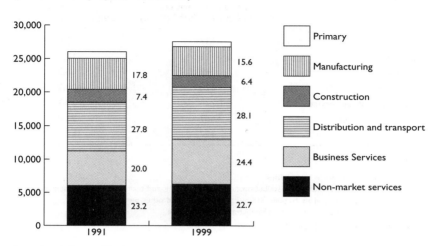

Source: Annual Census of Employment

growth has been very uneven. The business services sector has seen the biggest increase in employment, with the creation of over one-and-a-half million new jobs since 1991, a 29 %increase (see Figure 3.2). The other growth sectors have been distribution and transport (by 491,000), and non-market services (232,000). On the other hand, the manufacturing sector has seen the largest fall in employment – by 331,000 between 1991 and 1999. The primary sector has also seen a substantial decrease, reducing the number it employs by one quarter, or some 241,000 jobs.

However, these patterns of sectoral growth and decline vary across the regions. The primary and manufacturing sectors have seen decreases in all regions, while the business, distribution, and miscellaneous services sectors have seen increases in all regions. But manufacturing declined most in the North West, West Midlands and London while the reductions were rather modest in the South East, South West and East Midlands. The decline in construction, on the other hand, was most marked in London.

Business and miscellaneous services grew most in London and the South East – indeed between them they accounted for nearly 50% of total jobs growth in these sectors. On the other hand, growth in business and miscellaneous services was very modest indeed in the North East. Employment in non-market services (for example, education, health and public administration) grew in all regions, especially in the South West, Yorkshire, Humberside, the South East, and the West Midlands. The one exception was in London, where employment in non-market services actually declined.

If we examine sectoral trends at the more detailed level of the 17 Standard Industrial Classification categories, the most rapidly growing sectors have been business services (an increase of 43%); community/personal services (19%);

Table 3.1: Employment in the UK by broad sector (1999-2010)

	Change in numbers employed 1999-2010 (000s)	% share of employment in 2010
Primary	−137	2.0
Manufacturing	−713	12.1
Construction	+7	6.0
Distribution	+628	28.2
Business and other services	+1,774	28.7
Non-market services	+562	23.0
Total	+2,127	100

Notes:

Primary = agriculture, mining and utilities
Distribution = retail and wholesale distribution, hotels and catering, and transport and communications
Business = professional services, banking and business services and other personal services
Non-market = health, education, public administration and defence.

Source: Wilson (2001a, p 15, Table 3.2)

retail/wholesale (13%); and hotels/restaurants (12%). Conversely, employment in mining and quarrying has fallen by 48% and employment in the utilities (electricity, gas and water) has fallen by 37%.

At a more detailed level still, that of the 77 'SIC 2 digit' classification of sectors, we can identify the major changes within the manufacturing and services sectors. The main losses within manufacturing have been in textiles/clothing (a decline of over 20%) and metals. On the other hand, employment in rubber/ plastics and in electrical machinery grew – each by around one quarter. In services, the largest increases in employment have taken place in computing (which recorded an increase of 137%), refuse/sanitation, recycling, real estate activities and 'other' business services.

Further major changes in the sectoral composition of employment are expected to take place over the next decade (see Table 3.1). Over the period 1999-2010 it is anticipated that employment in the primary and manufacturing sectors will continue to fall. On the other hand, growth is anticipated especially in business and other services (up by over 1.7 million), non-market services (up by over half a million), and distribution (up by over 600,000).

These major structural changes in the economy and labour market have implications for the balance between full-time and part-time employment and for the gender composition of employment. In particular, the expected decline of employment in the primary and manufacturing sectors is likely to result primarily in the loss of full-time jobs, most of which have traditionally been held by men. In contrast, the growth of jobs in the various service sectors are likely to create more opportunities for women, particularly in part-time jobs, as the majority of these jobs have historically mostly been held by women.

Currently women account for 46% of total employment – 37% of full-time employment but 76% of part-time employment. Over the period up to 2010, while both male and female employment are expected to continue to increase, female employment is expected to grow more than three times faster than male employment. Male full-time employment is expected to fall, slightly, while female full-time employment continues to grow. The growth in part-time employment is also expected to be considerable, accounting for around three quarters of total jobs growth, and this growth is likely to be particularly rapid among males.

Occupational change

The most significant change in the pattern of occupations over the last decade has been the increase in the number and proportion of people employed in managerial and professional occupations. The proportion of people who are employed in these occupations has increased from 33% to nearly 37% of all jobs, an increase of almost 1.6 million people. On the other hand, the proportion of jobs accounted for by operatives fell from 25% to less than 22.5%, representing a decline of over 300,000 jobs.

An examination of recent patterns of occupational employment change based on the 25 SOC sub-major occupational groups (see Figure 3.3) shows the occupations in which the largest changes have occurred. Of the 1.6 million 'net' new jobs that have been created in managerial, professional and associate professional occupations, over 420,000 have been for corporate managers (that is, those working in managerial positions in the public sector, and medium and large-scale private sector organisations).

Business and public service associate professionals have also seen a significant increase, with 284,000 extra jobs, and there are now over 200,000 more science and technology professionals (for example, engineers and scientists) than there were in 1991.

Caring personal service occupations, such as childcare, healthcare and animal care, have experienced an addition of nearly 300,000 new jobs, a 41% increase between 1991 and 1999. The numbers employed in sales occupations have also increased substantially, with the creation of an additional 153,000 new jobs.

The most striking decline in jobs over the last decade has been in manual occupations. In 1991 some 56% of all jobs were to be found in SOC categories 5-6 (skilled trades and protective services) and categories 8-9 (plant and machine operators, drivers and elementary occupations) covering mainly manual occupations (both skilled and unskilled). By 1999 the proportion of employment accounted for by these jobs had fallen to 51%. This represents a net decline of over 600,000 jobs within these occupations with 248,000 being in skilled trade occupations. It is important to recognise however, that employment in these occupations still accounts for a substantial proportion of the workforce.

However, it is important to recognize that these occupational groups are all becoming increasingly qualified. For example between 1992 and 2000 the proportion of managers qualified to level 4 or above has risen from 26.1% to 37%. Equally it should be noted that not everyone in 'high skill' occupations are highly qualified. Even among associate professional and technical

Figure 3.3: Employment change by occupation, UK (1991-99, 000s)

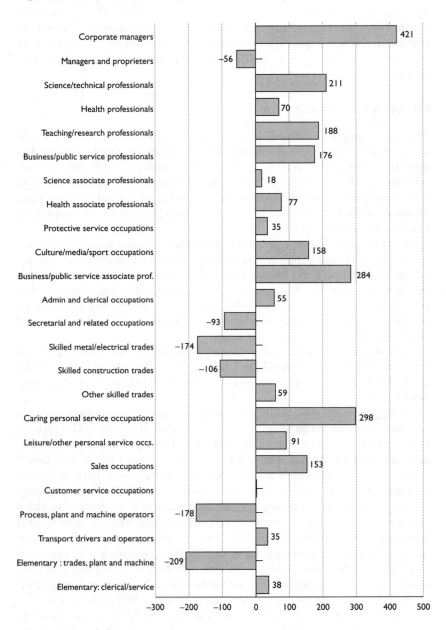

Source: Wilson (2001a, p 37, Table 43)

occupations, nearly a quarter of those employed (23%) do not have qualifications above level 2.

Regional patterns of occupational change

The patterns of occupational change that have been experienced have not, however, been consistent across the regions. For example, while the numbers of people employed as managers, and professionals are increasing across all regions, they are doing so particularly rapidly in London and the South East. Indeed, these two regions together account for almost 50% of the total increase in jobs in these occupations over the period 1991-99. On the other hand the increase in the North East is very modest indeed (Wilson, 2001b). The growth in associate professional and technical occupations is also concentrated in the South East and London with, again, only modest growth in the North East.

Skilled trades experienced a decline across all regions, except in the South East, while process, plant and machine operatives, and elementary occupations experienced their biggest losses in the North West and London. The latter's losses were most modest in the East and South East. Also, the number of jobs within both skilled and unskilled manual occupations have fallen across all regions since 1991, the only exception being within elementary occupations in the South East, which saw an increase of 10,000 jobs over the 1991-99 period.

Changes in occupational structure within sectors

These changes in occupational structure are associated partly with the major sectoral shifts that have taken place, but there have also been substantial shifts in

Table 3.2: Occupational structure – selected industries, UK (1991-99) (% of employment in the sector)

	Manufacturing		Distribution and transport		Business		Non-market		All	
	1991	1999	1991	1999	1991	1999	1991	1999	1991	1999
Managers	9.9	11.7	17.6	16.9	15.4	15.4	7.7	8.0	12.6	13.2
Professional occupations	5.2	6.3	2.2	2.6	11.2	13.5	21.5	24.7	9.3	11.1
Associate professional occupations	7.6	8.9	5.8	6.7	15.0	17.0	20.2	20.7	11.0	12.5
Administrative and clerical	9.6	9.0	11.4	10.7	29.4	25.5	17.4	15.5	15.7	14.7
Craft	26.2	24.4	14.1	14.0	5.4	5.0	2.9	2.4	15.5	13.7
Personal	1.1	1.3	2.5	3.0	5.3	6.7	11.0	13.2	4.6	5.8
Sales	1.9	2.0	18.1	18.7	3.2	2.9	1.1	1.0	6.4	6.6
Process	24.0	22.2	10.3	10.0	4.5	4.1	3.1	2.5	10.0	8.9
Elementary	14.6	14.1	17.9	17.4	10.6	9.8	15.1	11.8	15.0	13.5

Source: Skillsbase.dfes.gov.uk

occupational structure *within* sectors. Table 3.2 illustrates this in relation to the evolving occupational structure within the four largest sectors (in terms of employment) in the economy. The italicised entries indicate those occupations where the proportion of employment in the sector has declined over the 1990s. We can see that since 1991 all sectors, except distribution and transport, have seen an increase in the proportion of those employed in managerial occupations and all sectors have also seen increases in the proportion employed in professional and associate professional occupations. The business services and manufacturing sectors have experienced the most notable increases.

On the other hand, the proportion of craft and process workers employed has declined in all sectors, but it has been most marked in manufacturing. The decline in administrative and secretarial employment, by contrast, has occurred largely in business services and, to a lesser extent, in non-market services.

Future occupational trends

The occupational structure of employment is likely to change still further over the coming decade. What are likely to be the main trends in the future pattern of occupations? Figure 3.4 sets out the main changes. The occupations expected to show the most significant increases over the next decade are: professionals (+864,000); associate professionals/technical occupations (+789,000); and personal service occupations (+645,000). Smaller increases are expected for sales and customer service occupations (+178,000) as well as for managers and senior officials (+77,000).

For men, the biggest increases are in the professional and associate professional occupations while for women they are in the personal services, associate professional, and professional occupations. The occupations where the most significant reductions in employment are expected are in skilled trades (−196,000); process, plant and machinery operatives (−103,000); and elementary occupations (−177,000). Overall, these reductions affect women as much as men.

Within these broad occupational groups there are, however, considerable variations in the extent of jobs growth. For example, the particular occupations which are most likely to experience the fastest growth include: caring and personal services occupations; healthcare; business and statistical professionals; ICT professionals; childcare and related services; and leisure and travel service occupations (Wilson, 2001a).

These projected occupational trends are largely a continuation of trends over the last 20 years. Significant increases are being experienced in white collar, non-manual employment, especially in the service sectors, while blue collar, manual jobs, largely but not exclusively associated with manufacturing and primary sectors, have declined. There is one major exception to this long-running trend. Among administrative and secretarial occupations, developments in IT/computing are leading to a marked slow down in jobs growth compared to previous years, a process which particularly impacts on women.

Figure 3.4: Occupational change by gender, UK (1999-2010, 000s)

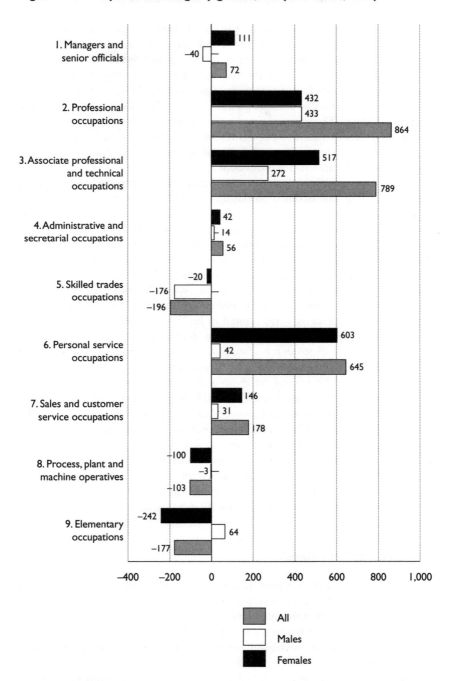

Source: Wilson (2001a, p 28, Figure 4.2)

Future regional trends in occupations and qualifications

Regional variations in the level and pattern of economic growth; variations in economic and occupational structures; and variations in qualification levels, will lead to major regional differences in future skill trends. Jobs growth is expected to be most rapid in the southern part of England with the four regions of the South East, South West, London and the East being likely to account for 70% of the expected additional 1.98 million jobs in England in the period to 2010. There is expected to be a particularly strong demand for managers in South East and eastern regions; for professionals in London and the South East; and for associate professional/technical occupations in the South East, South West and East (Wilson, 2001b).

These changes in the occupational structure are likely to lead to changes in the level and structure of qualifications that will be demanded across the regions. These very considerable differences in the pattern of employment growth across the various qualification levels are set out in Table 3.3. In relation to NVQ level 5 (higher degree) qualifications, the growth in employment at this level in the UK as a whole is expected to be around 31% over the decade. However, across the English regions this varies from highs of 37% in London and 34% in the East and South East, to just 20% in the West Midlands, and 21% in the North East, and Yorkshire and the Humber. Of all employment at this level in England, 47% is currently concentrated in just two regions – London and the South East, a proportion of which will rise still further over the next 10 years.

At NVQ level 4 (first degree or equivalent) qualifications, a similar pattern emerges but with even wider regional variations – from a 42% increase in London to just a 23% increase in the North East. In contrast, for those with NVQ level 3 as their highest qualification, London is projected to see a small absolute decline in numbers and there is also only a very modest growth in the North East. On the other hand, substantial increases are anticipated in the South East and the South West of around 14%.

At the same time, the numbers employed with no formal qualifications are expected to decline very significantly across all regions. Projected reductions in the number of employees with no qualifications range from over 40% in the West Midlands and 36% in the North West, to around 10% in the eastern region.

Replacement demand

Previous sections of this chapter have focused on the 'growth' and 'decline' of particular sectors, occupations and qualification levels. However, in addition to the changes in skill needs associated with the growth in new jobs, and the loss of old jobs, it is also necessary to 'replace' the skills that will be 'lost' as part of the normal process of labour turnover when people retire or change occupations.

Changes in the 'net' level of jobs take no account of the additional need to continually replace existing workers who leave an occupation through changing

Table 3.3: Projected employment by qualification (1999-2010)

Region	Level 5 1999 (000s)	Level 5 % change	Level 4 1999 (000s)	Level 4 % change	Level 3 1999 (000s)	Level 3 % change	Level 2 1999 (000s)	Level 2 % change	Level 1 1999 (000s)	Level 1 % change	No qualifications 1999 (000s)	No qualifications % change
London	328	36.9	1,123	42.4	615	-1.0	834	-9.7	802	-8.4	433	-25.4
South East	173	34.1	866	38.9	750	14.1	906	2.1	844	10.9	405	-17.8
East	100	34.0	468	38.5	445	8.8	592	5.1	564	9.6	271	-10.3
South West	92	33.7	499	33.1	440	13.6	533	4.1	511	12.9	236	-30.9
West Midlands	86	19.8	438	30.1	433	4.4	558	-0.7	541	10.2	390	-41.3
East Midlands	59	30.5	344	30.8	387	5.4	410	0.7	433	13.6	262	-26.0
Yorkshire & the Humber	86	20.9	436	26.2	402	6.7	496	-2.0	505	13.9	307	-25.4
North West	107	29.0	603	28.2	586	2.7	683	-1.8	618	7.6	383	-36.0
North East	29	20.7	184	22.8	204	0.5	237	0.0	230	11.3	141	-34.0
United Kingdom	1,237	30.8	5,864	33.2	5099	5.4	6,172	-0.9	5,778	8.2	3,388	-26.5

Source: Wilson (2001b, p 19, Table 14)

jobs or retirement. Even when net job losses are forecast for the future this does not *necessarily* imply that the total number of job openings or vacancies available to people will actually decline. Employers will still need to replace at least some of those workers who 'leave' due to retirement, career moves, mortality or other reasons. Indeed this 'replacement demand' may be quantitatively more significant than the 'expansion demand' which results from a net growth in employment in an occupational group. It may also outweigh negative employment changes resulting from projected employment decline in some occupations. Skills need to be available to replace the skills 'lost' through this process of labour mobility.

In a number of occupations – for example, managers and proprietors in agriculture and service industries; secretarial and related occupations; skilled metal and electrical trades; and plant and machine related workers – a large net decline in jobs over the next decade is expected to be more than outweighed by the volume of replacement demand (Wilson, 2001a). In other occupations, such as corporate managers; science and technology professionals; teaching and research professionals; health associate professionals; business and public service associate professionals; and sales occupations, the expected replacement demand will add to positive expansion demand to create even higher overall requirements for new entrants to the occupations.

The qualifications of the employed workforce

Clearly, all these changes in the sectoral and occupational structure of the economy are likely to have major implications for the qualifications of the workforce. For example, the proportion of those in jobs who were in possession of some sort of qualification rose from 75% in 1991 to 87% in 1999, while the percentage that held qualifications equivalent to NVQ level 4/5, rose from 17% to 26%. The proportion qualified to NVQ level 3 has also increased, while the proportions qualified to NVQ levels 1 or 2 have remained broadly similar. It is the proportion of the employed workforce that possess no qualifications which has declined most dramatically: it has nearly halved – from 25% to 13% of those in employment – in just 10 years.

All occupational groups are becoming more qualified, as measured, for example, by the proportion of employees qualified to NVQ level 3 (or equivalent) and above (see Figure 3.5). The increase is greatest among managers and clerical/secretarial occupations with a large increase also taking place among those employed in sales occupations.

The skill intensity of jobs growth

What of the future? The demand for skills is a function of both the changing occupational structure and changes in skill requirements within occupations. First, let us examine the impact of changes in occupational structure on qualification levels. Overall, jobs are growing in 'qualification rich' occupations and declining in 'qualification poor' occupations, a process which is driving up

Figure 3.5: Percentage of employees qualified to NVQ level 3 and above, by occupation, UK (1992-93 and 2000-01)

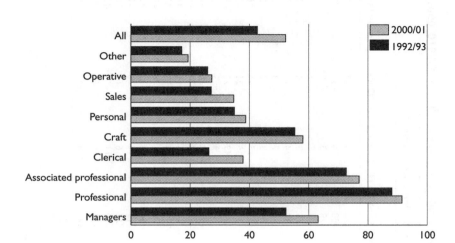

Source: National Statistics, Labour Force Survey (December-February 1993 and December-February 2001)

the overall levels of qualifications in the labour market. The future demand for qualifications depends on a combination of the changes that take place in the occupational structure and the changes that take place in the proportion of people employed in these occupations who require particular qualifications. Here we combine expected trends in occupational growth with the existing pattern of qualifications held, into a measure of the 'demand for qualifications' in order to provide an estimate of the likely skill intensity of future jobs growth (see Table 3.4).

The expected rapid growth in the numbers employed in several occupational groups where the qualification levels are relatively high (for example, corporate managers; professionals and associate professionals in particular) combined with the decline in several occupational groups (for example, secretarial and 'related' occupations; process, plant and machine operatives) where the qualification levels are relatively low, will, in itself, lead to an overall increase in the demand for higher level qualifications. Table 3.4 sets out the impact of projected occupational change on qualifications based on the assumption of a 'fixed' qualifications rate, that is, where the proportion qualified to the various levels in each occupation in the future remains at 1999 levels. In other words it assumes no increases in the proportion of people who are qualified to higher levels, over the next 10 years. In this sense the projected skill intensity of jobs growth is decidedly conservative.

Overall it is likely that 55% (1,151,000) of the new jobs that are projected to be created over the next 10 years, will be at NVQ level 4 or above; 24% (or 494,000) of the new jobs will be for those qualified to NVQ level 3; and 17% of the new jobs will be at NVQ level 2 or equivalent. The demand for those

Table 3.4: The skill intensity of jobs growth: projected change in demand for qualifications in the UK (1999-2010, 000s)

Occupation	Employment change 1999-2010	Change in demand for those qualified to				
		NVQ level 4+	NVQ level 3	NVQ level 2	NVQ level 1	No qualifications
Corporate managers	437	186	110	85	37	19
Managers in agriculture and services	-271	-49	-80	-64	-37	-40
Science/engineering professionals	149	106	28	8	5	1
Health professionals	91	82	1	1	7	0
Teaching professionals	166	154	5	3	4	0
Other professionals	340	266	34	24	14	2
Science/engineering associated professionals	60	30	18	7	3	1
Health associated professionals	59	50	4	3	2	0
Other associated professionals	509	232	123	93	45	16
Clerical occupations	147	21	34	56	21	15
Secretarial occupations	-113	-12	-22	-49	-22	-8
Skilled construction trades	22	1	10	3	3	5
Skilled engineering trades	-87	-11	-51	-12	-8	-6
Other skilled trades	-231	-61	-56	-53	-34	-28
Protective service occupations	94	5	44	15	15	16
Personal service occupations	858	115	294	253	133	63
Buyers, brokers/sales reps	-20	-2	-4	-6	-4	-3
Other sales occupations	196	50	54	62	17	13
Industrial plant/ machine operators	-64	-2	-15	-14	-16	-17
Drivers/mobile machine operators	35	1	8	6	15	5
Other farming occupations	-47	-3	-10	-11	-10	-13
Other elementary occupations	-247	-7	-33	-56	-61	-91
Total	2,082	1,151	494	354	131	-48
As a % of new jobs	100	55	24	17	6	-2
% of current workforce qualified to each NVQ level	–	26	24	23	15	12

Source: Policy Research Institute calculations based on IER Forecasts 1999-2010 and Labour Force Survey (Spring 1999)

without qualifications is likely to decline. Of course, the pattern of 'skill intensity' also varies considerably across occupations, as can be seen in the table, with, for example, the most rapid growth at NVQ level 4 being among 'other' professionals, 'other' associate professionals and among teaching professionals. At NVQ level 3 the growth is greatest among personal service occupations and 'other' associate professionals.

This rising 'skill intensity of jobs growth' assumes that there is no future increase in skill needs within occupations, as measured by employers' pattern of recruitment by qualification. If we were instead to extrapolate the trend in the proportions of people qualified to various levels at the rates of change that took place in the 1990s, the shift in the structure of demand towards those with higher levels of qualifications would be that much greater. For example, the fixed graduate qualification rate among corporate managers is 34.5% – the trend rate by 2010 (based on the growth of graduates in the occupation which was experienced in the 1990s) would be 44.6%; for 'other' associate professionals the respective ratios are 29.4% and 35.3% (Wilson, 2001a).

The evidence presented so far – regarding occupational trends and changes in the qualifications held by people in employment – suggests that skill levels have risen, that they changed quite substantially over the last decade and are likely to continue to do so. However, our review of occupational and qualification trends does not paint the whole picture of skill trends. While occupational trends refer directly to the jobs that people do based on a classification of skills levels, an increase in the actual stock of qualifications held by the employed workforce does not necessarily imply that these are actually required, or are appropriate, for the actual jobs that people do (Manncorda and Robinson, 1997). Moreover, the actual content of jobs (occupations) may have changed too – becoming more or less skilled. We now briefly consider these issues.

Over-qualification and over-education?

Trends in qualification levels may not give a wholly unambiguous guide to the changing skill needs of the labour market if one or both of two conditions hold. First, if the supply of more highly qualified people is not effectively absorbed into the labour market and actually utilised in the world of work, and second, if the jobs that people do, do not actually require the qualifications held in order to effectively undertake the job. Both of these conditions imply that there may be a growth of qualification attainment beyond actual qualification requirements. This would represent a waste of scarce resources devoted to the supply and acquisition of qualifications. Moreover, if the supply of more highly qualified people is not effectively absorbed into employment then this would represent a mismatch between labour market needs and people's qualifications, leading to structural unemployment and its potential coexistence with skill gaps and shortages (Campbell, 1993). And, if the jobs that people do, in reality do not actually require the qualification to undertake the job effectively, this may lead to 'bumping down' that is, the crowding out of less well qualified workers from particular jobs or the labour market more generally (Borghans and de Grip, 2000). So, is there evidence of the existence of such over-qualification of the workforce? Is there a 'skills surplus' caused by employers not actually requiring or utilising the skills that have been acquired and are thus available?

Elsewhere in this book we present evidence which suggests that there is a real, required skills upgrading taking place. In Chapter Four we identify earnings and employment differentials between high/low qualification workers; differing rates of return to various levels of qualification; and in this chapter we have seen a variety of indicators and evidence from the demand side, of a changing occupational structure. Furthermore, compared to other OECD countries for example, those with tertiary level education, enjoy an even higher wage premium and probability of employment in the UK (OECD, 2001b), implying a real need for higher skill levels.

In this section of the chapter we seek to provide evidence in relation to the two conditions set out above, that is, the absorption of qualified people into employment and the actual skill requirements of jobs.

First, are the newly available more highly qualified people being effectively absorbed into the labour market? A recent OECD report (OECD, 2001b, p 162, Chart C4.2) shows that the demand for highly qualified persons is in fact growing faster than the supply in nearly all OECD countries and, certainly doing so in the UK. The percentage point increase in the proportion of people with tertiary level qualifications in the employed population is increasing faster than the percentage point change in the proportion of people with such qualifications in the working age population. In the UK case, over the period 1989-96, the growth in the former was 7.5% compared to the latter's 6.4%. Demand is thus growing faster than supply.

Second, Green et al (2000) have examined the issue by asking people how necessary were the qualifications required of recruits for actually doing their job. An increased perceived necessity of the qualification would be evidence against the existence of over-qualification. They found that at NVQ level 2, there was an increase between 1986 and 1997, from 65% to 72%, of the proportion of people who indicated that the qualifications required in recruitment were indeed actually required to do the job effectively. At NVQ levels 1, 3 and 4/5 it actually, though only slightly, declined over the same period. Preliminary results from their follow up 2001 survey (Green et al, 2002: forthcoming) suggest that an increase, at least at level 4/5, has been experienced since 1997.

They also investigated, at three different qualifications levels, changes in the proportions of people who are employed in jobs where the qualifications that they hold are not required of those who are being recruited. Over the period 1986-97 there was a small increase at the highest level, stability at sub-degree level and a small decrease at lower levels. Furthermore, preliminary analysis of the follow-up 2001 survey suggests that the proportion of jobs requiring degree level qualifications is continuing to keep pace with the rising stock of degree holders in employment. They conclude that there is "no evidence of substantially rising over-education" (p 100); and that there is no major occupational group that has not experienced a demand for skill increases over the period 1986-97.

Overall then, the supply of more highly qualified people is being absorbed into employment, and the jobs that people do, generally appear to actually require the qualifications that people have acquired.

Trends in skill requirements

A range of related studies has recently shed considerable light on the skills actually used by the workforce (Green, 1999; Ashton et al, 1999; Felstead et al, 1999; Green et al, 2000). A major survey (henceforth 'the skills survey') was conducted in 1997 containing data on 2,467 people aged 20-60 who were in employment in 1997 that uses two sets of job based skills measures. Some of the results from this survey can be compared with other survey results from 1986 and 1992, where similar questions were used (Gallie, 1991, Green et al, 2000). An examination of skill trends between 1997 and 2000 will also soon become available (Green et al, 2002).

First, they sought to measure the abilities and capacities required for the job. They used three measures: (a) qualifications – what qualifications people possessed, what qualifications they would now require to get the same job and how necessary these qualifications were for doing the job competently; (b) training time – how long a period of training was necessary to undertake the type of work they were doing; and (c) learning time – how long would it take to do the job well. Skill trends over time can be examined by comparing the situation in 1997 with that in 1986 and 1992.

Second, respondents were asked to state their use of 'generic skills' – problem solving, communication skills, team working and computing skills – both now at the time of the survey (1997) and five years previously. Changes in these types of skills could thus be examined over the period 1992-97. We deal with each of the sets of findings on skill trends in turn.

In relation to the abilities and capacities required for jobs, the 1997 skills survey found that between 1986 and 1997 the proportion of jobs that required some form of qualification had risen from 62% to 69%. For high level (above 'A' level) qualifications the proportion rose from 20% to 24%, and for degree level, from 10% to 14%. The proportion requiring no qualifications fell from 38% to 31%. On this measure, overall skill requirements have clearly risen.

One way of measuring skills actually utilised in a job is the level of qualifications that is both required of new recruits and which is also regarded as necessary to do the job. On this measure too there has been an increase in skills required – again at all qualification level except at NVQ level 3. It is important to note that these skill increases are, however, more pronounced for women than men.

With regard to the training and learning time measures, there has been a decrease in the proportion of workers whose type of work requires only a short (less than three months) training period from 66% to 57%. There has also been an increase in the proportion of jobs with long (more than two years) training requirements, from 22% to 29%. Additionally, there has been a fall in the proportion of jobs which respondents judge take only a short time (less than one month) to 'learn to do well', from 27% to 21%.

It is also the case that women's skill levels have, on these measures, been catching up with those of men – although they still remain at a lower level. Moreover, the up-skilling is not particularly concentrated among younger members of the employed workforce, which might be expected due to the considerable rise in the qualifications level of young people joining the workforce over the period. Skills, on a wide range of measures (required qualifications, prior training and time to learn job) have increased as much, if not more, among those age 35 and over (Green et al, 2000, pp 88-9).

Turning to the trends in skills required within occupational groups, Table 3.5 sets out the results for the six skill measures they used. For every occupational group there is an overall increase in skills in every occupation – although not on every measure. The highest rates of skill increase were in 'personal and protective services' occupations. Training and learning times increased in all occupations.

We now turn to generic skills. The abilities demanded by different jobs vary enormously, and to capture this diversity, the 1997 skills survey included questions on a broad range of different job activities, and respondents were asked how important each job activity was in their current job. In order to address the question of how job demands had changed over recent years, respondents were asked a number of repeat questions about the job they held five years before the date of the survey. The questions focused on skills related to problem solving, communication and social skills, manual skills and computing. By comparing the average importance ratings given for activities carried out in jobs occupied in 1992 with those for the same activities five years later, it is possible to track trends in these particular skills.

Table 3.6 summarises the main results. For all problem solving skills, all communication and social skills, and all computing skills, the proportions of respondents reporting a higher level in 1997 compared to five years earlier, exceeded those reporting lower levels by a substantial margin. Counting each move up or down the skill 'scale' as one, the third column presents the average 'change' in position, which is also positive for all these skills.

On the other hand, with respect to manual skills, the proportion reporting a decrease exceeds those reporting an increase and the 'average change' column shows a significant reduction in usage. The changes in all four skill 'sets', problem solving, communication, manual skills and computing skills, applied to both men and women.

How have these changes in skill attributes and generic skills been distributed across the workforce? Felstead et al (2000) have shown that, in terms of the abilities and capacities required for the job (skill attributes), there has actually been a reduction in workforce skills inequality both between men and women and across occupations. The highest level of skill increase has in fact been in 'personal and protective services' occupations. However, part-time and temporary workers and those working in 'traditional' organisations (in terms

Table 3.5: Skill trends by occupation (%)

Occupation	Requiring any qualifications	Using degrees	With low prior training	With high prior training	With short time to learn job	With long time to learn job
Managers and administrators				**	*	
1986	78.8	13.0	55.9	28.8	14.5	32.1
1997	78.5	17.0	51.8	32.4	5.8	39.5
Professionals			**	**		
1986	97.2	45.4	46.5	36.7	6.7	49.8
1997	98.2	49.9	32.2	54.1	5.7	51.5
Associate professionals and technicians	**	**	*		**	
1986	86.3	11.9	41.3	41.0	13.0	39.7
1997	89.6	20.4	34.4	43.9	5.7	36.7
Clerical and secretarial		**	**	**		
1986	78.4	1.2	72.0	11.4	21.1	10.1
1997	81.4	3.0	65.2	17.1	19.6	9.4
Craft and related			**	**	**	
1986	68.1	1.5	54.1	36.2	15.2	39.7
1997	72.3	1.9	42.1	45.3	7.3	41.1
Personal and protective service	**	*	**	**	**	
1986	33.2	0.0	77.0	14.0	48.1	16.4
1997	59.1	0.9	55.5	23.4	30.3	14.1
Sales occupations			**	*		*
1986	31.7	1.8	89.0	6.3	49.0	7.6
1997	37.6	1.4	81.7	11.9	44.5	3.5
Plant and machine operatives				*		
1986	41.9	0.4	80.7	10.1	36.1	16.8
1997	43.1	0.0	77.8	15.5	38.3	13.3
Other occupations						**
1986	16.1	0.9	92.8	4.2	63.4	2.0
1997	20.3	0.0	89.4	7.2	58.9	6.0

Notes: Significance levels for difference between 1986 and 1997: * = 10%, ** = 5%

Source: Green et al (1999, p 91, Table 4.7)

Table 3.6: Type of work skill changes in Britain (1992-97, %)

Skill type	Increasing[a]	Decreasing[a]	Average change[b]
Problem-solving skills			
Spotting problems or faults	34.6	20.4	0.25
Working out the causes of problems or faults	36.7	20.2	0.29
Thinking of solutions to problems or faults	34.1	19.9	0.25
Analysing complex problems in depth	39.3	18.6	0.37
Communication and social skills			
Dealing with people	34.7	12.6	0.34
Instructing, training or teaching people	46.7	17.3	0.62
Making speeches or presentations	31.9	12.4	0.27
Persuading or influencing others	36.4	21.8	0.25
Selling a product or service	29.4	20.1	0.20
Counselling, advising or caring for customers or clients	36.9	24.6	0.45
Working with a team of people	34.9	27.8	0.27
Manual skills			
Physical strength	20.7	27.3	-0.12
Physical stamina	20.2	31.0	−0.20
Skill or accuracy in using hands or fingers	23.1	29.0	−0.10
Computing skills[c]			
Using a computer, PC, or other types of computerised equipment	42.0	10.4	0.63
Level of computer usage	29.2	6.1	0.27

Notes:

[a] Work skills were self-assessed by job-holders against the 5-point scale: 'essential/very important/fairly important/not very important/not at all important or does not apply'. A skill increase or decrease is defined as a move up or down) one or more points of this scale between 1992 and 1997.

[b] Calculated as the average number of places moved up or down the skill response scale. A positive figure means a skill increase, while a negative figure means a skill decrease.

[c] Assessed on a scale: 'straightforward/moderate/complex/advanced', using examples.

The base is all those who were in employment both in 1997 at the date of interview and five years earlier.

Source: Green et al (2000, p 95, Table 4.9)

of human resource practices), compared to 'modern' work organisations, have seen their skills grow less quickly. This is suggestive of a link between the way in which work is organised and the nature of skills required, such that work itself may facilitate or inhibit skills development. There is, however, one area where skill inequalities are rising. In relation to computer use, those at the higher occupational levels are increasing their computer skills faster than those at the lower levels.

In summary, our assessment of occupational and qualification trends that have occurred in the 1990s and those that are likely to occur over the next few years, provides substantial evidence of a significant increase in skills demand. In addition, the findings of the Skills Survey in relation to job attributes and generic skills also show a consistent, clear pattern of increasing skills utilisation in the UK. To this evidence we can add the existence of important skill shortages and skill gaps, discussed in the previous chapter, which provides additional evidence and articulation of a skills imbalance between the skills that we posses and those that we need.

Conclusions

The labour market, and the skills required in it, are changing very considerably as a result of changes in the pattern of consumer demand, globalisation, and information and communication technologies, or as it is sometimes put more generally, the ' three T's ' – tastes, trade and technology.

A substantial proportion of the new jobs being created will be in relatively few sectors of the economy – most notably business services, health, education, distribution and hospitality. Occupationally, growth continues to be in the 'white collar' jobs – caring and personal services; business and public service professionals and associate professionals; corporate managers; and teaching, research and technology professionals.

Jobs are growing in mainly 'qualifications rich' occupations with more than half of new jobs growth over the coming decade likely to be at NVQ level 4, with particularly strong expansion here among corporate managers, and professionals and associate professionals. It will be necessary to 'drive through' people's skills progression from NVQ level 2 to NVQ level 3 and from NVQ levels 3 to 4, in order to effectively meet this evolving demand. Moreover the substantial variations in the evolution of skills across the regions needs to be recognised – in terms of matching skills supply effectively to these needs. But this also has to be addressed as a problem, which requires action on both the supply and demand sides. As well as meeting the skill needs of 'new' jobs it is also important to make skills available to replace the skills 'lost' through retirements and occupational mobility.

A range of 'skill types', which cut across occupational, job specific, skills are also of considerable importance. These include: generic skills requirements such as problem solving; communication and team working skills; the basic skills of literacy and numeracy; and IT skills, from basic IT literacy through to advanced computing skills and management skills.

New times require new skills.

FOUR

The value of skills

"Education is the best economic policy we've got." (Tony Blair)

Introduction

Are skills valuable? Do increasing skill levels benefit the people, organisations and communities who acquire them? Do they increase peoples' employment opportunities? Do they increase peoples' earnings potential? Do they enhance organisational effectiveness and profitability? Do they stimulate the economic performance of communities and the economy as a whole? In previous chapters we have examined the current supply of skills, and the deficiencies that exist in the skills base we possess. We have also assessed the pattern of evolving skill needs: the skills that are required to meet the changing needs of the economy and labour market. We would expect from this assessment that improvements in skills supply are necessary to meet, and to keep pace with, the pattern of skills demand. The market for skills is 'signalling' that more people with higher level skills are needed and that there are insufficient skills available. Market failures also mean that insufficient skills are developed to meet actual and potential skill needs. We would expect to find, therefore, that skills are indeed valuable.

It is important to assess the value of skills not only because this will provide an evidential base for assessing the economic significance of skill formation, but also because the evidence can be utilised in pursuit of the encouragement of skill acquisition. In a real, material sense, people, organisations and communities need to be convinced of the economic benefits that can accrue from raising skill levels in order for them to be persuaded so to do. The 'incentive' to acquire skills, if it exists, needs to be identified and effectively communicated so that individuals, employers, learning providers and public agencies can respond to the signals being provided.

The first part of the chapter considers the benefits of skills acquisition for individuals. The second part examines the benefits to companies. Finally, we consider the wider benefits to the overall economy and its constituent communities.

Individuals

There is a strong relationship between the qualifications people possess and their earnings (see Figure 4.1). The chart shows the average earnings of people

Figure 4.1: Average earnings by highest qualifications held, England (1999)

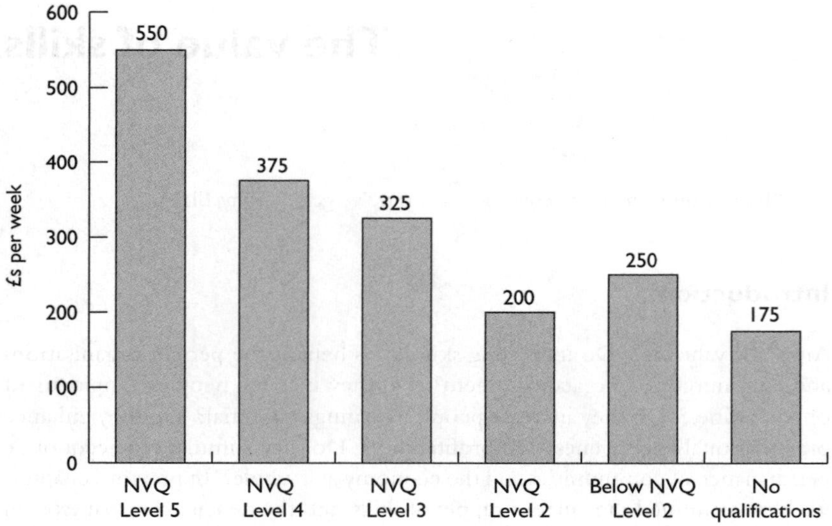

Source: Labour Force Survey (Autumn series 1999)

qualified to different levels in England. Overall, the more highly qualified people are the higher their earnings are. For example, the average earnings of those who possess NVQ level 5 qualifications is over £900 per month higher than those who have 'A' Level or other NVQ level 3 equivalent qualifications – a premium of 70%. Similarly the earnings of those qualified to NVQ level 3 exceed those of people without qualifications by around £600 per month – a premium of 85%. It is only at NVQ level 3 and above that people's earnings rise above the average. It is, however, important to note that the earnings of those at NVQ level 2 are somewhat below those who have level 1 qualifications (NACETT, 2001).

Another way of obtaining a broad indication of the earnings premium associated with higher level qualifications is to compare the gross lifetime earnings of people with different qualifications (*The Guardian,* 15 January 2002). For example, the national average gross lifetime earnings for a full-time employee amounts to around £686,000. For someone with a first degree the comparable earnings amount to £1,071,000 – an earnings premium of £385,000 or 56%. This substantial premium is even higher for women (a 62% premium) than for men (a 50% premium).

This positive link between earnings and educational attainment is, in fact, common across most OECD countries (OECD, 2001a, p 299ff), although the earnings benefits associated with higher level qualifications are particularly high in the UK. The relationship between qualifications and earnings for prime age men and women (30- to 44-year-olds) across the OECD countries

Figure 4.2: ILO unemployment rates by highest qualifications held, England (1999)

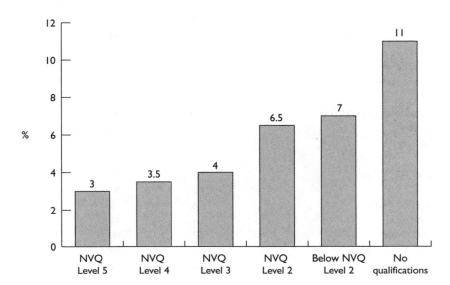

Source: Labour Force Survey (Autumn series 1999)

(OECD, 1998) shows that the premium for women of securing a degree compared to upper secondary level qualifications in the UK is 110% – the highest in the OECD. Their premium for securing upper secondary qualifications over no qualifications, while still important, was much lower at 20%. For men, the premium of securing a degree relative to upper secondary level qualifications in the UK is 65% – one of the five highest in the OECD. The premium for securing upper secondary level qualifications over no qualifications was, as with women, still important, but much lower at 25%.

There is also a strong link between peoples' qualification levels and their likelihood of being unemployed (see Figure 4.2). The chart shows the unemployment rate for those qualified to different levels in England. It is clear that unemployment rates vary systematically by qualification level. The greatest improvement is associated with acquiring NVQ level 1 and NVQ level 3 qualifications (NACETT, 2001). A recent OECD study (OECD, 1998) demonstrates that across a wide range of countries, those with higher levels of education face lower risks of unemployment. Indeed, the 'gap' in the expected number of years of unemployment (for example, for men) is greater in the UK than in any other OECD country – 5.4 years for those with below upper secondary level attainment compared to 2.8 years for those with upper secondary level attainment and 1.6 years for those with tertiary level qualifications. As with earnings, the employment benefits of acquiring qualifications are considerable.

Table 4.1: Wage premia from obtaining qualifications (%)

Qualification	Men	Women
CSE/lower GCSEs	9	5
O level/higher GCSEs	21	19
A level	17	19
First degree	28	25
Higher degree	8	18
Professional qualifications	35	41
Nursing	13	21
Teaching	Nil	27
Level 1-2 NVQs	Nil	Nil
BTEC First	Nil	Nil
Level 3-5 NVQs	6	5
RSA Higher	4	12
C&G Craft	7	Nil
C&G Advanced	7	Nil
ONC/BTEC National	10	8
HND/HNC	15	9

Notes:

[1] The wage premiums are additive. For example, a man with 'O 'levels/higher GCSEs and 'A' levels and a first degree will earn 66% more than a man with no qualifications.

[2] Results control for age, ethnicity, region, firm, size, public/private sector.

Source: Dearden et al (2001)

A range of generic skills are also highly valued by the labour market (Green, 1999). In particular, computer skills are highly valued, even at moderate levels of complexity, with workers commanding a wage premium (after controlling for other factors, including education) of around 13% compared to those who do not use computers. Professional communication skills and problem solving skills are also highly valued.

Analysis of rates of return data across a range of countries shows that the 'returns to schooling' (the number of years spent in full- time education) in the UK are the second highest (around 8%) in the sample of 16 countries studied (Harmon and Walker, 2001). The rates of return were found to be highest for those who earn most and were also quite considerably higher for women than for men. After extensive examination of various estimation methods, the authors conclude that "there is ... an unambiguously positive effect on the earnings of an individual from participation in education".

More specifically, we can examine the returns to different levels and types of qualification. Dearden et al (2000, 2001) have assessed the returns to a range of UK qualifications as well as those to basic literacy and numeracy (see Table 4.1). The key findings are that the returns to academic qualifications are high at

NVQ levels 2, 3 and 4. GCSEs/'O' levels produce a return of 21% for men and 19% for women. 'A' levels produce an additional 17% for men and 19% for women, while first degrees produce a further 28% for men and 25% for women. These wage gains are additive. Thus, for example, men acquiring 'A' levels earn on average around 38% more than those without any qualifications. The returns to most professional qualifications are also very high, with the notable exception of teaching for men. The returns to higher level vocational qualifications (ONC/HND/HNC) are also high. However, lower level vocational qualifications do not appear to yield a significant return, and the return to NVQ qualifications appears to be relatively low. However, when consideration is given to the time required to obtain the qualifications, the returns per year of study to vocational qualifications at NVQ levels 3 and 4, are in fact broadly similar to academic returns.

These estimates of rates of return do not, however, provide information on subjects of study and so are unable to shed light on which specific skill areas generate the highest rates of return. They do, however, give an indication of the levels of qualification where the market appears likely to reward any future additional supply.

It is not only relatively high levels of qualifications that generate a return to people. Dearden et al (2000, 2001) have shown that the returns to acquiring basic literacy and numeracy skills are also high, in terms of both earnings and employment rates. They find a large positive impact on earnings in respect of numeracy at 'entry' level and NVQ level 1. The effect of enhanced literacy skills on earnings is similarly large. The effect on employment is also positive for both literacy and numeracy, with a possibly larger effect for literacy than numeracy.

Indeed, individuals with level 1 numeracy skills earn around 15-19% more than those with skills below this level. Even after controlling for qualification level and family background the wage premium is still between 6-7%. Moreover, individuals with level 1 numeracy skills are around five percentage points more likely to be employed. Individuals with level 1 literacy skills earn around 15% more than those without skills at this level and are around five percentage points more likely to be employed.

Bynner et al (2001) show that, after controlling for family circumstances and educational achievement, level 1 and above numeracy and literacy skills (key skills) produce respective returns of 26% and 16% compared to adults with skills below these levels. The probability of employment is also considerably enhanced.

This work on rates of return to basic skills acquisition corroborates the observation that the earnings of people with high levels of literacy/numeracy substantially exceed those with low levels (Moser, 1999). Table 4.2 shows the substantial differences in earnings levels with, for example, 49% of those with low levels of literacy and 55% of those with low levels of numeracy earning less than £9,000 per annum, compared to 23% of those with high levels of literacy and 16% of those with high levels of numeracy.

There are also considerable earnings gains associated with training (for a

Table 4.2: Earnings of people with different levels of literacy and numeracy

£ per year	Literacy		Numeracy	
	Low level[a]	High level[b]	Low level[a]	High level[b]
<9,000	49	23	55	16
9,000-13,000	27	16	22	17
13,000-19,200	17	20	15	21
>19,200	7	40	7	48

Notes:

[a] 'Low' level = IALS level I

[b] 'High' level = IALS level 4/5

Source: Moser (1999, Table 3.1)

review of the evidence see Machin and Vignoles, 2001). One recent major international study (OECD, 1999) demonstrated that the earnings gain for trained workers was particularly high in the UK – most especially for women and those educated to less than upper secondary level (OECD, 1999, p 164). The UK evidence more generally shows a positive return to training individuals similar in scale to that for education especially for those with pre-existing lower levels of educational attainment (Blundell et al, 1996). Individuals undertaking employer provided vocational training typically earn around 5% higher earnings in real terms than those who have not undertaken such training. The returns increase to up to 10% if the training results in a middle or higher level vocational qualification. Typically the returns also tend to be higher for women, and for training which is off- the-job (Blundell et al, 1999).

Qualifications and occupations of the unemployed and the economically inactive

An important aspect of understanding the value of skills is to consider the skills of the unemployed – in particular those of the long-term unemployed and the economically inactive. When such skills are compared to those of the currently employed this provides a picture of 'redundant' skills: those that are in excess supply in relation to labour demand, those indeed for which there is, by definition, not a current demand. This is the other side of the coin, the mirror image, of the premium attached to higher level skills and the increasing demand for certain occupations. We saw in Chapter Two that the qualification levels and occupational background, of the long-term unemployed and the economically inactive are markedly different from those who are currently in employment. The most notable difference between those in employment, and those that are either long-term unemployed or economically inactive, is that those in employment are much more likely to have higher level qualifications (NVQ level 3 and above), and individuals that are long-term unemployed or inactive are much more likely to have low level qualifications (NVQ levels 1 or

2), or no qualifications at all. There exists therefore a considerable excess supply of those with no qualifications, of those with NVQ level 2 qualifications and, to a lesser extent, those with NVQ level 1 qualifications.

If we compare the previous occupation of the long-term unemployed and the economically inactive with the present occupation of those currently in work, we find that while nearly two fifths of those in employment are in managerial, professional and technical occupations while only one fifth of the long-term unemployed and the economically inactive were formerly in these occupations. On the other hand, before they ceased being employed, just over one third of the long-term unemployed and a quarter of the economically inactive were in non–craft related manual occupations, whereas currently these occupations only account for 15% of employment. This suggests that the excess supply is greatest among plant and machine operatives, 'other' elementary occupations and craft occupations. Their skills need to be markedly improved if they are to benefit from the ongoing process of economic change and not to be left behind as a result of the constant evolution of the labour market.

So, this issue is of importance to the unemployed and the economically inactive themselves, in terms of their prospects of accessing the evolving pattern of labour market opportunities, and it is also important to the economy as a whole, because they represent a potential, but currently unused, source of labour supply.

Companies

How far do skill levels affect company performance? A literature review of over 20 studies on the effects of enterprise training on company performance across a range of countries commissioned by CEDEFOP concludes that: training has a positive effect on productivity; training received by people from one employer increases their productivity with another subsequent employer; but the type of training is important to outcomes as is its combination with other human resource policies and practices (Barratt et al, 1998).

One means of identifying the contribution of skills to company performance is to compare companies on the basis of 'matched' samples. A series of detailed comparative studies, at the level of the organisation, provides evidence of the linkages between learning and organisation performance. Studies of comparable plants between the UK and elsewhere, demonstrate that a large part of the UK's lower productivity is due to deficiencies in the skills of its workforce (Prais, 1995; Mason et al in Booth and Snower, 1996; Green and Steedman, 1997). Productivity gaps of between 25% and 60% exist in matched samples of organisations in the engineering, clothing, furniture, food processing, and hotel sectors of the UK economy compared to those in Germany, France and the Netherlands. These productivity differentials have been found to be largely the result of differences in skill levels/vocational qualifications between the organisations in the UK and those elsewhere in the European Union, rather than differences in capital equipment. The main reason for higher output per employee in similar plants in the same sector of the economy was the qualifications and skills of the workers.

A study by Mason and van Ark (in McNabb and Whitfield, 1994) comparing matched samples of UK and Dutch engineering plants found that output per hour worked was 25% to 30% less in the UK than in the Dutch plants and that this was due, in large part, to lower levels of workforce skills in the UK. Mason et al (1994) have also found that in matched sample comparisons of biscuit manufacturing in France, Germany and the Netherlands, where capital equipment was roughly equivalent, compared to the UK, quality adjusted productivity was between 25% and 40% higher than in the UK. This difference was found to be largely attributable to the lower levels of qualification of UK workers and to less effective 'on-the-job' training.

A report on the role of employers in lifetime learning (Metcalf et al, 1994) shows that companies that trained more tended to be more successful. Of all employers studied, 94% saw lifetime learning as advantageous to their productivity; to workers motivation; and to improved working relations.

Another comparative study between the UK and Germany shows that the skills gap in manufacturing is a major factor in explaining the UK's relatively poor trade performance: the larger the skills gap in any sector, the worse is the UK's export performance compared to that of Germany (Oulton in Booth and Snower, 1996). The main deficiency was found to be in craft and technical skills. Closing the skills gap by 1 percentage point would, it is estimated, be able to improve UK exports by 4.3% relative to those of Germany.

A further long-term comparative study between the UK and Germany (O'Mahoney et al, 1994) reveals that productivity growth was greatest in those industries where the proportion of workers with higher level skills was highest. The study also revealed a positive correlation between productivity growth and intermediate level skills (the disparities in qualifications are very considerable especially with regard to intermediate level qualifications). Those industries where the proportion of skilled workers was rising between 1979 and 1989 were those that experienced the fastest productivity growth.

There also appears to be evidence of a strong connection between training and productivity. An increase in the sector wide training rate of 50% (say from training 10% of workers to 15% of workers) is associated with a 4% rise in productivity as measured by value added per worker. Moreover, the productivity effect seems to be more than twice as high as the effect on workers wages (1.6%), thus demonstrating the benefits of training to employers as well as individuals (Dearden et al, 2000). Other studies show a higher return on training when it is associated with a wider 'bundle' of human resources practices (Blundell et al, 1999).

Cosh et al (2000) demonstrate a positive impact from training on jobs growth in small and medium size enterprises with, again, a 'wider bundling' of human resource practices increasing the effect. Patterson et al (1997), in a study of 67 companies, found that nearly one fifth of both productivity and profitability differences between them were associated with differences in human resources practices in general, and skills development in particular. A note of caution, however, is provided by Green (1997) who, reviewing around 20 studies of the impact of training, found little UK evidence on a positive impact of training in productivity or profitability.

A series of case studies which considers employers' own views about the impact of training on their organisation's performance provides qualitative evidence in support of the quantitative studies outlined above (Campbell et al, 2000).

Another means through which the value of skills to companies and other organisations can be identified is to consider the negative consequences of the existence of skill deficiencies, in the form of skills shortages and skill gaps, on organisational performance.

Skill shortages, skill gaps and organisational performance

An insight into the extent to which the existence of skill shortage vacancies affects organisational performance is contained in Hogarth et al (2001). Overall, just over one third (34%) of establishments that report the existence of skill shortage vacancies say that it has led to a loss of business or orders to competitors; nearly half of them (49%) indicate that it has delayed the development of new products; and just over half (51%) indicate that it has led to difficulties with customer service.

It also seems to be the case that certain occupational skill shortages are more associated with negative performance than others. Skill shortages in skilled trades appear to have the greatest negative impact − both in terms of the proportion of organisations affected and the range of problems which they give rise to.

Skill shortage vacancies among senior officials and managers, and in professional occupations, also appear to give rise to serious consequences both in terms of the proportion of organisations affected and the range of problems which they give rise to. Shortages in associate professional/technical, and in operative occupations appear to have a negative effect, mostly on the development of new products and on customer services respectively.

In terms of the sectors of the economy in which skill shortage vacancies appear to have the most negative impact on performance, those most negatively affected are the manufacturing, construction and finance sectors − again both in terms of the proportion of establishments affected and in the range of impacts across various measures of organisational performance. For example, in manufacturing, half of those establishments experiencing skill shortages report a consequent loss of orders, and six in ten (59%) report delays in developing new products.

There are significant negative effects in all other sectors too − being perhaps most extensive in public administration, education, and health and social care. In each of these three cases, around half of establishments report difficulties with customer services as a result of skill shortages.

Skill shortages can also impact negatively on wage inflation pressures and productivity growth with consequent negative effects on the economy. Haskel and Martin (in Booth and Snower, 1996) estimate that skill shortages in the UK economy in the 1980s reduced annual productivity growth by around 0.4% and raised wages growth by around 1% per year. They also demonstrated that most skill shortages related to skills deficiency rather than the failure of companies to adjust wage levels to the evolving pattern of skills supply and demand.

We can gain an insight into the extent to which the existence of skill gaps impact on organisational performance through the work of Hogarth et al (2001). The main effects of skill gaps overall are associated with difficulties in customer service, quality, increased costs, and problems with introducing new working practices – each of these occur in more than one third of establishments experiencing skill gaps.

Unlike the situation in respect of skill shortages, where there is no apparent relation between their impact and size of establishment, the impact of reported skill gaps does appear to increase with size of establishment. The sectors of the economy, in which skill gaps appear to have the greatest negative impact on performance, are manufacturing, transport, finance and public administration.

Latent skill gaps and performance

As we saw in Chapter Two, latent skill gaps constrain the potential for economic growth and are therefore of considerable importance. Their existence provides evidence of a 'low skill equilibrium' (see Chapter Five) where organisations are not demanding the skills that are actually required to achieve enhanced organisational success. While in practice latent skill gaps are difficult to measure, recent research results (Bosworth et al, 2001) suggest that the incidence of skill gaps would rise by around 2.5 percentage points, or some 10%, and the incidence of skill shortages would increase by around 4.2 percentage points, or almost one third.

Latent skill gaps show just how important the 'demand side' is in understanding skills problems. Employer skill requirements are structured by their business strategies – their approach to product, service and process innovation, and to organisation growth and development more generally. Some strategies can lead to a pattern of workforce skill requirements which, while broadly appropriate to *current* needs, do not provide a basis for long term enhanced competitiveness or performance through adaptation to changes in technology or the market place (NSTF, 2000a). Latent skill gaps are gaps that need to be filled if the UK is to develop as a high skill, high value added economy and their existence is an indication of the benefits that could accrue to parts of the corporate sector if a 'higher skill' route was chosen by more companies.

The economy

If skills are able to contribute to both individual and corporate economic well-being, it may be thought likely that they would enhance national economic performance as well as doing so in those communities which have relatively high skill levels.

Long-run studies do indeed tend to show a considerable contribution of education to economic growth in the UK (OECD, 2001). Psacharopoulos (1985) estimates a contribution of between 12% and 19% for the period 1945 –84, while Sturm (1993) estimates it to be around 19% for 1973-84. Jenkins (reported in Blundell et al, 1999) suggests that a 1% increase in the proportion of workers with higher qualifications raised annual UK output over the period 1971-92 by between 0.42% and 0.63%

Across the OECD countries it has been found that differences between countries in the 'stock' of human capital are an important factor in explaining observable differences in economic growth (OECD, 2001, pp 48ff). Indeed, apart from trade exposure, it is probably the single most important explanatory variable in determining why economic growth rates differ between OECD countries. For the UK, certainly, it is the single most important variable in explaining the growth of GDP per head in the 1980s and 1990s.

Other studies provide further evidence of the contribution of skills to economic performance. According to one recent study based on a sample of countries, a one percentage point increase in school enrolment rates tends to generate economic growth of up to three percentage points. An additional year of secondary level education for the population as a whole would have the impact of increasing economic growth by an additional one percentage point per year (Sianasi and Van Reenan, 2000). A study by Englander and Gurney (1994) showed that the enrolment rate in secondary education added 0.6% points to annual productivity growth across the OECD countries over the period 1960 to 1985. In each decade of the 1960s, 1970s, and 1980s, they found that educational attainment is one of only three variables which have a robust correlation with productivity growth.

Communities

There is some evidence available on the economic benefits of learning for localities. This issue is of importance, not only to the communities themselves, but to the way skills development is delivered, given the geographical focus of much policy and action.

A study for the National Skills Task Force (Campbell, 1999, 2002) provided evidence of substantial variations in skill levels across England. For example, the proportion of the workforce who have no qualifications varies from a high of 20% or more in places like Easington, Walsall and Tower Hamlets to a low of 5%, or even less, in places like west Devon, Reigate or south Cambridgeshire. At the other 'extreme' some counties, like Humberside and Cleveland, have less than 20% of their workforce qualified to NVQ level 4 while others, like Oxfordshire, Surrey and Buckinghamshire, have more than 30% of their workforce qualified to NVQ level 4.

The study also examined the relationship between these variations and a range of indicators of local economic performance. Overall, the results show an association between a wide range of measures of local skills levels – in the form of the proportion of the workforce qualified to various levels – and patterns of employment growth, competitiveness (as measured by GDP per head), earnings and deprivation. The study provides extensive evidence of the relationships between skills, economic performance and social inclusion at the local level; and a summary of the findings here will serve to illustrate the value of skills to localities as well as the difficulties associated with localities where skill levels are low.

There is a positive correlation between jobs growth, across the 46 English counties, and the qualifications of the counties' workforce as measured by the proportions who are qualified to each of NVQ levels 2, 3 and 4. The closest association (r=0.45) is with the proportion of the workforce qualified to NVQ level 2. Jobs growth across the counties varies from a decline of 13%, between 1991-96, to a growth of 11%; and the proportion qualified to NVQ level 2 varies from a low of 65% in Humberside, Cumbria and the West Midlands, to nearly 80% in Cheshire.

In terms of the relationship between GDP per head, which varies from a high of 144% of the UK average in London to 71% of the UK average in Cornwall, and the proportion of the workforce qualified to each of NVQ levels 2, 3 and 4 across the counties, again there is a positive association – with the strongest being in respect of the proportion qualified to NVQ level 4 and above (r=0.65).

Average earnings also vary considerably across the counties. For example, average earnings in Buckinghamshire (the county with the highest level of average earnings) are 50% higher than in Cornwall (the county with the lowest level of average earnings). Again, there is a close relationship between average earnings and the proportions of the workforce qualified to each of NVQ levels 2, 3, and 4. The highest correlation (r=0.7) is with the proportion qualified to NVQ level 4 and above.

At the local level we can reasonably conclude that there are strong links between skill levels and a range of indicators of economic performance. The very existence of 'skill rich' and 'skill poor' localities has important implications. Such inequalities restrict many individuals life chances and the scope for competitive advantage for many companies. They also hinder the prospects for a sustained growth in skill levels at the national level. There are economic costs associated with being a low skill locality and considerable economic benefits associated with being a high skill locality. Skill rich localities are almost always rich localities.

A recent study by the OECD (OECD, 2001c) provides further evidence of the links between skills acquisition and economic growth, this time at the regional level, across the 15 EU member states. A correlation analysis between three measures of educational attainment and GDP per capita across the 180 EU regions "a significant correlation between GDP per capita and the primary and secondary level indicators, though the relationship with tertiary level education is weaker". In other words there is a close association between regional economic performance and the qualification levels of the regions' workforce, as measured by the proportion qualified to NVQ levels 2 and 3. It appears, however, that the association is weaker in terms of the proportion qualified to NVQ level 4 and above. It is important to note though, that the results of the study for the English regions show a strong relationship at this level as well.

Conclusions

We can reasonably conclude from this review of the evidence on the value of skills, that skills are indeed highly valuable – to people, to companies and other organisations, to the country as a whole and to its constituent communities.

Indeed, the value of skills appears to be particularly strong in the UK. It really does seem to be the case that' learning pays'. People's employability is enhanced and their earnings are increased. Companies' productivity and business performance are enhanced. This evidence needs to be publicised effectively to those who are able to influence the decisions of individuals, employers and public agencies who are engaged with skills issues. Careers advisors, adult guidance workers, the new Sector Skills Councils, Regional Development Agencies and, in particular, Learning and Skills Councils are all critical to this process and need to be galvanised in the process of stimulating the demand for skills.

Skills development can, then, make an important contribution to both the economic and social policy agendas. It can help to enhance economic performance – through raising people's productivity (and hence their earnings), through improving company (and other organisations) performance, and through making a positive contribution to the local, regional and national economy. But its contribution to tackling social exclusion is also important. It enhances people's employability, improves their access to job opportunities, and raises their incomes, even with relatively modest improvements in skills levels. As a sign once read on the City Hall in Gary, Indiana: "beat poverty – get educated". A skills revolution would indeed be a key route through which 'opportunity for all' can be effectively delivered.

FIVE

An agenda for action

"Philosophers have merely interpreted the world. The point, however, is to change it." (Marx)

Introduction

We have established a powerful economic and social case for skills acquisition. The value of learning is considerable. We have also seen how the need for skills is increasing and that our skills base is weak in a range of ways. This is our 'interpretation' of the skills 'world'. However, such knowledge needs to be put to use to 'change' the skills world, through developing an agenda for action which would seek to markedly improve our skills position. There is a case for policy action by government to tackle a range of skill deficiencies, in order to ensure that the UK has the skills base necessary both to compete effectively in the modern world and to secure access to economic opportunities for its citizens.

Indeed, the government has recently established (in April, 2001, for England) the Learning and Skills Council whose goal is precisely to raise attainment and participation so that "by 2010 young people and adults ... will have knowledge and productive skills matching the best in the world" (LSC, 2001). They have set five key objectives to this end:

- extend participation in education, learning and training;
- increase the engagement of employers in workforce development;
- raise achievement of young people;
- raise achievement of adults;
- raise the quality of education and training.

Furthermore, the government is establishing, in April 2002 with UK-wide coverage, a new network of Sector Skills Councils (SSCs) to replace the existing National Training Organisations. A new Sector Skills Development Agency will be established to develop and monitor the SSCs, whose remit is to:

- reduce skill shortages and skill gaps;
- improve productivity and human performance through targeted interventions to tackle specific sector priorities;
- increase the proportion of the sectors' workforce participating in training and in the level of training investment.

In this way it is expected that the role of employers in skill formation will be increased, the 'demand' for skills increased and the responsiveness of the supply side increased.

This chapter sets out a range of proposals which, if adopted, could assist the Learning and Skills Council and the SSCs, as well as others such as the Regional Development Agencies and their partners, through their new 'frameworks for employment and skills action' in securing the challenging goal of building a 'high skill' society which is both competitive and inclusive. The chapter proceeds as follows. First, it identifies, on the basis of evidence and argument presented in earlier chapters of this book, a range of skills issues which ought to be treated as priorities for action. Second, it sets out the main barriers or challenges that policy makers and practitioners face and which need to be overcome in engineering the skills revolution that is required. On this basis we then go on to set out the main means through which such barriers can be effectively overcome. Finally, we conclude by making a plea to 'connect' this skills agenda to wider economic, employment and social policy agendas.

Priorities for action

We can identify eight priorities which, taken together, constitute a challenging but necessary agenda for change (Campbell et al, 2001; Cabinet Office, 2001).

Learn to succeed

There are substantial economic benefits that accrue from skills acquisition. Individuals, companies, communities and the country as a whole all benefit when people increase their skill levels. Higher skills levels are required for the jobs of the future because while the new jobs that are being created are predominantly 'skill rich' the jobs that are being lost are predominantly 'skill poor'. The message that we must 'learn to succeed', that it pays to learn, to train and to acquire qualifications, must therefore be promoted as a key means of stimulating the demand for learning among individuals. The message that 'learning matters' to companies – to their staff's productivity, commitment and, above all, to the company's economic performance – also needs to be promoted to generate a step change in the number of companies who effectively invest in their people. The Sector Skills Councils have a crucial role here. Increasing skill levels contributes to both the competitiveness and social inclusion agendas, as organisational and economic performance improves alongside the enhanced earnings and employability of those individuals who acquire the additional skills.

Encouraging both participation and progression in learning ,through linking it to the likely economic benefits that accrue to its participants, provides the foundation for marketing learning in terms of the benefits it can bring to people and organisations. Such an approach would encourage people to participate in learning, to 'consume it' if you like, in the way that marketing strategies operate in respect of other 'desirable' products and services – by focusing on the benefits it brings as well as on the characteristics of the product itself. Education and training are excellent 'products' but they have been badly sold. Individuals and employers will, on the whole, only purchase things if they have an incentive to do so, and believe that there are, or are likely to be, demonstrable benefits to them. The same logic applies to government and public agencies – they will, rightly, only prioritise skills if it can be shown that skills development 'works' in helping to achieve government or agency objectives.

Thus, the evidence base – changing labour market and skill needs as well as the economic benefits that accrue from learning – needs to be marshalled, publicised, and communicated effectively and persuasively. Of course, our research evidence is limited and needs further development. Indeed, investing in this research base is likely to pay handsome dividends in helping individuals, employers, and public agencies, as well as those who advise them, in making sensible, well informed decisions with respect to investing in learning.

The bottom line is this. If people and employers are not persuaded of the benefits of learning, it is likely that insufficient skills will be developed to create a more successful and cohesive society.

Balance skills demand and supply

It is important to seek to ensure that the *pattern* of skills which is being acquired 'matches' the changing requirements of the labour market. In other words we need to balance the skills we have available with the skills we need. There is no point, from an economic or social point of view, in raising skill levels beyond that which is required, in terms of the volume of people or in terms of the level of skills they acquire. This will only lead to the non-fulfilment of people's aspirations and expectations. It would also represent a waste of the individual, corporate and state resources that are deployed in acquiring those skills. Similarly, the existence of an excess demand for skills is inefficient, in bidding up the price of skills in short supply, in leading to skills shortages and gaps, and to negative economic consequences on productivity and competitiveness. In many cases, of course, the market will balance skills demand and supply with individuals and companies responding to the economic signals of earnings, employment prospects, productivity and so on – especially if the relevant information signals are made available and effectively transmitted to those concerned. However, public agencies will also need to monitor labour and learning market conditions for signs of *skills mismatch* – skill shortage vacancies in particular occupations or at particular qualification levels; shifts in the pattern of (the previous) occupations and qualifications of the unemployed; changes in occupational wage differentials; and changes in the employment destinations and employment success rates of those leaving education and training.

It will also be necessary for the Learning and Skills Council to encourage providers of education and training, through information, incentives and the planning of provision, to seek to ensure that the pattern and level of provision evolves in a manner that reflects ongoing changes in skill needs. Local LSCs will, in particular, need to find effective ways of funding those providers and courses which are likely to be of most benefit to local economies and communities.

The continuing structural changes in the labour market mean that a large proportion of 'new' jobs are likely to be in a relatively small number of occupations and that many of these jobs will require higher levels of qualifications than are currently available. In parallel, a range of jobs will be lost in other occupations, often with relatively lower qualifications levels. It is important therefore to monitor evolving supply patterns and their interaction with the pattern of skills demand, at national, as well as sectoral, regional and local levels, so as to ensure that no major imbalances develop. It will also be important to encourage labour market adaptability among the workforce and to encourage appropriate skills acquisition decisions, through information and incentives, in a manner which is consistent with evolving labour market demands. This again requires ongoing research and intelligence at the national, regional and local levels.

Raise skill levels and participation in learning

Overall, qualification levels are rising but a number of serious problems remain to be tackled effectively. First, there remains a relatively high proportion of the workforce who have either no qualifications or qualifications below NVQ level 2 and too many women do not progress effectively from NVQ level 2 to NVQ level 3. Second, attainment levels are highly uneven across the workforce with the unemployed, economically inactive, older workers, those employed in manual occupations and some minority ethnic groups – most notably people of black, Pakistani and Bangladeshi heritage – possessing low levels of educational attainment (Cabinet Office 2001b). Minority ethnic groups will account for more than half of workforce growth in the next decade and, as such, enhancing their qualification levels is of particular importance. Third, there remains a relatively low proportion of young people who participate in full-time education and training. Despite progress in recent years, participation remains very low by international standards. Finally, overall adult participation in learning appears to have reached a plateau in recent years. In particular, it may be that participation by young people in higher education, after many years of continuing increases, has ceased to expand.

Actions to raise attainment and widen participation in education and training are of considerable importance.

Skill deficiency 'hotspots'

There are a number of particular concentrations of skills problems where attention is required. Here we suggest five possible areas for action.

Skill shortages

These affect around one quarter of employers with vacancies and their specific nature and distribution across sectors, localities, size of establishment and occupations, as well as their economic impact, makes them of particular importance. Action is particularly urgent with regard to small enterprises, and the construction, manufacturing and business services sectors.

Information, communication and technology skills

The most sought after skills in the main skill shortage occupations are advanced ICT skills and there continues to be substantial increases in the demand for, and use of, computer skills which also continue to attract a high wage premium (Green et al, 2001, 2002). The ICT sector itself, as well as the demand for ICT professionals, has also experienced considerable growth in recent years.

Management skills

Management occupations are one of the most rapidly growing groups in the workforce. Moreover, increasing numbers of other employees undertake a range of management tasks. The nature of the skills required by managers is also changing rapidly. Most important of all, it is management in organisations who are responsible for decisions on skills acquisition.

Intermediate level skills

Associate professional and skilled craft occupations together account for nearly one fifth of total employment. They typically require qualifications at NVQ level 3 and there is a good deal of evidence which imply a shortage of these skills. First, the highest proportions of skill shortages are in these two occupation groups. Second, international comparisons show that in terms of literacy and numeracy at IALS level 3 (defined as a suitable minimum for coping with the demands of everyday life and work in an advanced society) the UK is lagging behind most OECD countries. Third, the rate of return to vocational qualifications at level 3, at least for males, is high. More generally, the earnings levels and unemployment rates associated with the acquisition of NVQ level 3 qualifications show a significant improvement over those associated with NVQ level 2 qualifications. Finally, there is projected to be a continued substantial expansion of demand for associate professional jobs, as well as significant replacement demand for skilled craft workers.

Generic skills

These are skills that can be used across a range of occupations and, as such, are transferable. Employer surveys continually draw attention to the importance of these skills and the wide extent to which they are sought (see Hogarth et al,

2001; Baldwin et al, 2001). Evidence relating to the skills actually utilised by the workforce also demonstrates upward trends in the use of problem solving, professional communication, writing, and in particular, computing skills, in recent years. The demand for these generic skills varies by occupation and is particularly strong in the professional, associated professional ,and technical and managerial occupational groups.

Sustained action to tackle these five skill priority areas would go a long way to resolving many of the more immediate skills problems.

The role of employers

Employer awareness of skills issues and their responsiveness to them is critical. Recruitment and training decisions, attitudes to product and service development, and their commitment generally to investing in people, can make a significant difference to the volume, nature and distribution of skills across the workforce. Three particular aspects need to be more seriously addressed: their *provision of training*; the extent of *skill gaps in their workforce*; and their *recognition of the existence of latent skills gaps.* The new Sector Skills Councils will need to place these issues at the forefront of their plans.

Workforce training

Training is an important means through which skills acquisition can be increased. Workplace training has increased in recent years, but access to it is unevenly distributed among the workforce with semi- skilled and unskilled manual and service workers, the less well qualified, part-timers and older workers being among those least likely to receive training. Moreover, the size of an establishment is an important influence on the level and type of workplace training provided, with smaller establishments being less likely to provide formal workplace training than larger ones, especially with regard to off-the-job training. The distribution of training thus reinforces existing differences in skill levels.

Skill gaps

There is evidence of the existence of skill gaps in the workforce: a situation where there is a divergence between an organisation's current skill levels and those required to meet organisational objectives. The main skill gaps, in terms of the skill characteristics that are lacking, are: advanced and basic IT; communication skills; technical/practical skills; team working; customer handling; and problem solving skills. The sectors most affected by skill gaps are manufacturing and hospitality, and to a lesser extent wholesale/retail, financial services and public administration. Nearly half of skill gaps in manufacturing relate to production/process operatives and around 40% of skill gaps in financial services and public administration are in administrative/secretarial occupations. Nearly 40% of health and social care skill gaps are in personal service occupations.

These skill gaps negatively affect organisational performance in a range of ways – customer service, quality, costs and new working practices in particular. Of course, one important cause of the existence of skill gaps is a failure by employers to train staff in the first place.

Latent skill gaps

Some skill gaps may not be recognised as such until the organisation tries to improve its position in terms of growth or market position. As organisations try to 'raise their game' and perform in line with the 'best' in their sector, new skill gaps are revealed. Moves to higher value added production or services provision, expansion into new markets or shifts in technology or organisation, uncover additional skill requirements, including those necessary to achieve these changes and improve organisational performance. Their existence provides evidence of a 'low skill equilibrium' There is a need to make employers more aware of the importance of skills for their long-term success and to assist them in addressing these 'hidden' problems. Moreover, these latent skill gaps demonstrate the importance of the product and service strategies which employers pursue in structuring the demand for skills. Certain strategies may lead to a pattern of workforce skill requirements which possibly may be appropriate to employers' current needs but do not provide the basis for longer term enhanced competitiveness or performance.

Regional and local differences

There are considerable regional and local variations in many elements of the demand for, and supply of, skills, as well as in the extent and nature of skill shortages and skill gaps. It is essential that these differentiating features are articulated, recognised and responded to by providers and agencies as well as by individuals and employers, because the skills issues confronting different areas are often different in scale and nature. There is also a danger that the skill problems will not only affect local and regional economic performance and social exclusion, but also national economic performance and social inclusion, as a result of the combined existence of 'skill rich' and 'skill poor' areas. This is because it will be very difficult to secure a substantial and sustained improvement in skills performance without significant improvements in currently skill poor regions and localities. This is likely to involve the stimulation of skills demand as well as skills supply.

Inequality and social inclusion

Skills are unequally distributed across various groups in the population. Because of the importance of the possession of skills to both individual labour market success and social inclusion it is important to recognise the existence of such widespread skill inequalities and to develop a sustained attack on them. There are perhaps four key dimensions of these inequalities, which the LSCs in particular need to urgently address.

First, in terms of the *attainment of qualifications*. Around 30% of the workforce either have no qualifications or hold qualifications below NVQ level 2. Attainment levels are highly uneven across different social groups, with the unemployed, the economically inactive, those aged over 50 and those employed in manual occupations among the groups who are least likely to hold any formal qualifications. Well over a quarter of the long- term unemployed (29%) and nearly 40% of the economically inactive have no qualifications at all. In particular, certain minority ethnic groups are disproportionately unlikely to hold any qualifications – people of Bangladeshi, Pakistani and African Caribbean heritage groups are particularly disadvantaged in this regard. Their attainment levels are of particular importance in localities where they constitute a large proportion of the actual and potential workforce, for example, London.

Second, *poor basic skills* are a significant problem. Around 1 in 5 adults have lower levels of literacy than that expected of an 11-year-old: nearly half have lower levels of numeracy than that expected of an 11-year-old; and there may be as many as seven million adults who could be considered functionally illiterate or innumerate. This lack of basic skills impacts on people's employability and earnings potential yet a relatively small proportion of those who lack basic skills currently admit to recognising that they have literacy or numeracy problems.

Third, *participation levels* in post-16 education need to be increased in order to raise attainment and reduce inequalities in skills levels. The proportion of young people participating in education post 16 has increased considerably over recent years but compared to most OECD countries young people's participation in full- time education is low. Participation rates in higher education have grown only slowly in the late 1990s. Moreover, participation in adult learning has failed to increase in recent years and nearly 40% of adults have not participated in learning since they completed their full time education. Most importantly, there are significant disparities in participation rates in learning across different groups, with particularly low levels evident among older workers, the economically inactive, those in skilled, semi and unskilled manual and service occupations, and those who completed their initial education at the earliest age.

Fourth, while there has been a substantial growth in *workplace training* in recent years, access to such training is unevenly distributed among the workforce. Certain groups, most notably plant/machine operatives and those in elementary occupations, the less well-qualified, part-time workers, older workers, and those working in small establishments are least likely to receive training. This inequality in training participation is cumulative – those who do not receive training in one year tend also to be excluded from it in future years.

International comparisons

It is important to position the main dimensions of our domestic skills performance in an international context. This helps to benchmark and map progress, not just against our domestic past, but through an assessment, in relative terms, against our European Union and OECD member nations. While substantial improvements have taken place in our skill levels in recent years, these generally look much more modest when they are held up against a mirror of the skill performance of other countries. As competitiveness is relative, a regular international benchmarking study to identify areas of relative strength and weakness,, would be useful.

One final point needs to be established. It is essential that the skills agenda simultaneously addresses all three components of the potential workforce – those who are currently employed; new entrants to the workforce (from schools, colleges and universities) and re-entrants to the workforce, in the form of women returners, the unemployed and the previously economically inactive.

Tackling barriers

In tackling the priorities set out in the previous section and in developing an agenda for action, it is essential to identify, and address, the main reasons why individuals and employers do not acquire sufficient skills. What prevents them from investing sufficiently in learning? There are two sets of challenges. The first relates to the operation of the market – there may be 'market failures' which operate so as to make it difficult for some individuals and employers to acquire sufficient skills. The second relates to the personal, institutional or policy barriers which operate in a similar manner. Many of these market failures and barriers are discussed in more detail in Ashton and Green (1996); Campbell (1995); and Keep and Mayhew (1996), but we outline the major market failures and other barriers in turn here.

We have already dealt, in a different context, with a key cause of market failure – insufficient, inadequate or inaccessible information on the benefits (and costs) of skill acquisition. If people and organisations are poorly informed then action is required to improve information in terms of availability, accessibility and quality. Markets work poorly if information is limited as the signals for action are not clear (NSTF, 1999; Cabinet Office, 2001). If the incentive to learn is insufficiently known about then individuals, employers and providers will make incorrect decisions. In particular, if the returns to learning, to general and specific levels, and types of qualifications and courses are not known, there will be general under investment in skills acquisition as well as both under and over investment in particular levels and courses. Moreover, there may be asymmetries of information between individuals and employers with employers having certain skills requirements which are imperfectly known by employees. Our own recent skills audit work (Baldwin et al, 2001) confirms the existence of such asymmetries with regard, for example, to the need for enhanced generic skills. Furthermore, a lack of, or asymmetry in, information

Figure 5.1: A low skills equilibrium

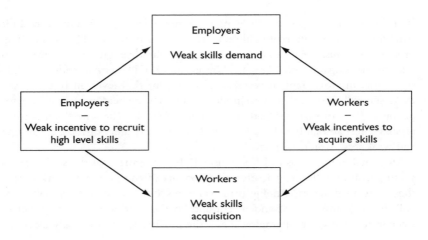

can create uncertainty for prospective learners in terms of the likely pay off from their learning decisions – that is, earnings, jobs and so on.

It is, therefore, crucial to enhance information, advice and guidance services, for both young people and adults. The new Connexions Service, in the former case, and the developing Information, Advice and Guidance (IAG) partnerships have crucial roles to play here.

A second key cause of market failure is the existence of what is often referred to as the 'poaching externality' (Booth and Snower, 1996). If the benefits of skill acquisition cannot be fully 'captured' by the individual and/or employer concerned ,then insufficient skills will be acquired. This situation arises in the following way. If the training which takes place is useful only to someone's current employer ('specific' training) then the benefits accrue only to that employer and the employee. If the training is useful to all employers ('general' training) the benefits accrue largely to the worker. However, as most training is actually useful to a *range* of employers it is, if you like, 'transferable' rather than specific or general. Under these conditions workers are unable to appropriate all the returns, as they could if the training was general. Because they change jobs/employers, the benefits of the training accrue to the current employer *and* to any other employer who can make use of it. Employers thus have less incentive to contribute than they have with specific training as they do not reap all the returns. So, as the worker and current employer, between them, cannot appropriate all the benefits, they are likely to under invest. What is more, some employers, who we can term 'poachers', will recognise that they will get some of the benefits of the training without providing it, as they can obtain it 'free' when they recruit workers from the previous employer. It is therefore, important to provide incentives for employers to fund, undertake and provide such training, perhaps on a 'collective' basis in a locality, sector or across relevant occupations.

There is also the related issue that as labour markets become increasingly flexible, and the average duration of peoples' spells of employment with a given employer diminish, then the incentive for employers to train a given individual will similarly diminish, as the period in which they can expect to reap a return will decline. This, increasingly, transfers the decision to learn, as well as its costs and benefits, to individuals.

A third dimension of market failure relates to the situation where it is possible for the interaction of weak skills supply *and* weak skills demand, to generate a 'low skill equilibrium' where there is little incentive to raise skill levels (Snower, in Booth and Snower, 1996; Finegold and Soskice, 1988). We illustrate this problematic situation in Figure 5.1. The 'problem' can begin at any point in the cycle.

Employers may have a low demand for skills initially, either because in their locality the level of available skills is low *or* because they have adopted a low skill method of production or service provision. Indeed the employers may have located there specifically for these reasons. Workers in the locality will, as a result, have no incentive to acquire more skills as these are not required. Employers will have no incentive to adopt different methods of production or service provision. Moreover, potential employers who are relocating will be 'attracted' by the existing configuration of skills, ensuring that there is no incentive through inward investment to change the skills base. Thus, in certain localities, sectors of the economy, or types of enterprise, a situation can develop where employers and workers get 'locked' into a low skill equilibrium where there is no incentive to raise skills levels. The market for skills may be in equilibrium but the locality, sector, employers and workers are trapped in a low skill, low value economy – what has also been referred to as a 'low skill-bad job' trap (Snower, in Booth and Snower 1996).

This issue demonstrates the importance of recognising the interdependence of skills demand and skills supply and the consequent need for action on *both* simultaneously. A skills equilibrium, where there are few skill shortages or gaps, may hide an underlying problem. However, it does need to be established where the critical deficiencies 'originate', as it will be of little use stimulating demand, if the supply is not forthcoming. Nor will it be of much use if supply is activated but the demand does not exist. The issue also draws attention to the role of business strategy more generally, in structuring the 'initial' demand for skills in the workforce. In this regard it should be recognised that skill shortages are greatest in localities of high skills demand and high skill levels, rather than in areas of low skills demand and low skill levels (Green and Owen, 2001).

Tackling a low skills equilibrium will require simultaneous action on both the demand and supply sides with, in the former case, industrial and competitiveness policy playing a key role in encouraging employers to adopt product and service strategies which require a highly skilled workforce, and, in the latter case, encouraging them to develop their workforce skills. In this regard the LSC and the SSCs have crucial roles to play in preparing workforce development plans and in working with the Small Business Service to encourage commitment to 'Investors in People'. The task is to create a 'high skill equilibrium', where both supply and demand conditions are strong.

We now turn to the other, non-market, barriers that face those making skill investment decisions. We deal first with individuals and then with employers.

For many people who are already working in formally structured occupational and internal labour markets there is a strong incentive to learn (Finegold, 1991; Chapman 1993). Here, progression and mobility depend in part on continuous learning; employers and professional associations often have well structured learning programmes and there is often a culture of lifelong learning. However, for people who work in so called 'secondary' labour markets – many part-time workers; those on temporary or short term contracts, and many of the self employed – both employer and individual incentives to upskill are limited by the availability of clear career progression routes and by high levels of labour turnover. Here, both organisational and personal 'cultures' do not always value learning. Moreover, in many cases the costs of skill acquisition can be high relative to earnings, which are often low. There is therefore a need to assist people in such labour markets through targeted interventions in order to encourage skills acquisition, for example in the form subsidies (for example, individual learning accounts or tax relief) or even a 'right' to learning/ qualifications up to a certain level (Cabinet Office 2001a).

The provision of learning opportunities is also an important issue. Provider flexibility is important in respect of being able to match the times at, and locations of, which people are prepared to learn, as well as in the forms that people find accessible and attractive. Rigid provision, in terms of times of the year and times of the day, as well as rigid thinking in terms of the types of place and location in which learning takes place, can be an important barrier, in particular with regard to people with young children, elderly/sick dependents, older relatives, and people who work non-standard hours. For many, particularly for those whose experience of school was poor, locating facilities in schools or classroom type environments is a strong disincentive. The use of ICT can also be important, for example in developing 'distance' learning and in providing an attraction, especially to young people, who find internet use stimulating. A commitment to accredit prior learning and a willingness to provide (and assess and accredit) learning in 'bite size' chunks are also likely to be important to many people.

Related to the issue of flexibility is the problem of the availability of time which continually shows up in surveys as the single greatest barrier for many people. This refers not only to the opportunity cost of people's discretionary leisure time, but to the difficulty of obtaining permission from some employers to engage in learning during working hours.

Another issue is that of the cost of learning, not only in terms of fees and materials but also in the form of earnings foregone (especially if the provision is on a full-time basis). Raising finance for learning can be difficult because of the 'moral hazard' facing financiers (where the potential increase in earnings is controlled by the learner not the financier), and the problem of 'adverse selection' facing both financier and learner, that is, where an individual's background may lead some to question their likelihood of success. Young people face the additional problem of lack of financial collateral and lack of credit history. In such circumstances subsidised loans or grants may help overcome these problems (as government does, to an extent, for first degree provision) providing they do not distort the pattern of provision across levels. They could, however, be used to encourage types and levels of skills acquisition consistent with evolving labour market needs.

There are also some barriers on the demand side which constrain the ability to reap the full returns from skills acquisition, of which two are of particular importance. Limited geographical mobility reduces the range of employment opportunities open to people, particularly if they are currently living or working in 'job poor' localities. Such immobility reduces the range of opportunities open to people to enhance their skills and hence their potential earnings/employment gain. Secondly, discrimination may restrict the returns to a range of people – some people in minority ethnic groups, older workers, and women, inter alia, may not achieve their full potential because of conscious or unconscious discrimination or stereotyping. They will thus be 'under-employed' and prevented from fully using their skills. It follows that encouraging geographic mobility to areas of employment opportunity, through commuting or migration, and measures to tackle labour market discrimination and stereotyping, can increase the incentive to acquire, and subsequently to realise, the benefits higher level skills.

As far as employers are concerned we have already drawn attention to the problem of 'poaching' and of the potential existence of a low demand for skills because of the pursuit of a wider business strategy which does not require high skill levels. These apart, employers, like individuals, face the problem of time constraints – individuals engaged in many forms of learning incur an opportunity cost on employers, at least in the short run. 'Time off' and reduced staff availability and flexibility are especially a problem in small organisations. Additional problems include management skill levels, the lack of recognition of the long term benefits of investing in workforce skills and the complexity of government policies, incentives and funding regimes: all of these may operate so as to constrain, especially small scale employer, skill investment decisions. In these cases, it is particularly important to 'make the case' for skills, in terms of the direct benefits to employers and to seek to change the culture away from employers seeing learning as a 'cost' to seeing it as an 'investment'. The increasing importance being attached to knowledge management in an era where creativity and innovation are important competitive advantages may help to encourage some employers, as would the development of strong, relevant role models and the encouragement of a high skills strategy by relevant employer organisations and by the new Sector Skills Councils.

It is also important to recognise that investing in workforce development is often neglected in the development of business strategies. Less than two fifths of companies have training plans and less than a quarter have human resource development plans (Spilsbury, 2001). Even when it is not neglected it may be that some members of the workforce lack the motivation to engage in learning.

A quarter of adults have not undertaken any kind of learning in the past three years and half of those who say that they have undertaken no learning in the past 10 years say that 'nothing' would encourage them to learn (DfEE, 1997).

Finally, it is important to recognise that skill formation – like the economic performance and social inclusion that it seeks to foster – is not solely shaped by the kind of 'technical' policy actions set out above. They are also socially and politically constructed (Brown, Green and Lauder, 2001). Moreover, there is also a potential relationship between building social capital and the development of human capital (OECD, 2001) through the generation of cooperative behaviour and trust relations between the various networks engaged in the skills agenda. The specificity of economic conditions, the cultural attitudes and mores of the key interest groups, and political conditions will also influence the skill formation process. Brown, Green and Lauder (2001) consider how a *societal* capacity for 'high skills' can be built, developing its institutional foundations and relations of trust between the key actors, by identifying an 'ideal type' of the societal conditions which are most likely to stimulate high skills. They refer to this as the 'seven Cs' of high skills:

- consensus: consensus between the major stakeholders to skill upgrading;
- competitive capacity: high potential for innovation through entrepreneurial endeavour linked to new technologies and skills upgrading;
- capability: an inclusive approach to the way people think about their abilities and those of others whereby all are seen to have the potential to benefit from skill upgrading;
- coordination: a recognition that the demand for skilled labour matters as well as the supply of skilled labour, so encouraging means to match the needs of the economy with rising skill levels;
- circulation: the means by which skills upgrading is diffused beyond the 'best' firms, sectors and localities;
- cooperation: the existence and stimulation of high levels of trust in the institutional fabric of society;
- closure: a commitment to address exclusion in both skill formation and its utilisation on the labour market; skills for the many, not just for the few.

A focus on these societal and political conditions will be of great importance in developing the necessary environment within which a skills revolution can be effectively developed, nurtured and sustained. Above all, this involves a deep societal commitment to recognise, accept and adapt to change. As Bill Clinton has observed, perhaps the most urgent question of our time is, "whether we can make change our friend and not our enemy".

Joining up the policy agenda

Finally, it is essential to recognise that the skills agenda needs to be connected to other policy agendas. There is considerable potential for synergy between policies. The learning 'market' is, in large part, driven by the labour market, in terms of employment opportunities and earnings, and the labour market is, in turn, driven by the economy. The alignment of economic, employment, and education and training policies is thus important. It is essential, in this context, to ensure that actions to tackle social exclusion across the different policy fields are also connected together so as to make them consistent with each other. Signals are transmitted and behaviour is influenced across these spheres. Conflicting signals, or the lack of signals, reduces information and knowledge and makes it difficult for 'correct' decisions to be made. The consequences of poor decisions are then felt more widely. Policies therefore need to point in the same direction – they should all seek to encourage higher levels of skills formation. This sounds like common sense but, as Voltaire remarked, "common sense is not so common".

To illustrate the considerable importance and implication of this point let us briefly take the example of local economic development policy (Campbell, 1995). A wide range of initiatives can be taken at the local level in pursuit of economic development and, it is important to ensure that they all signal a 'high skills' orientation. For example:

- inward investment – a focus on potential investors, sectors and types of activity which embody relatively high skills levels will be important; for example, relatively routine assembly operations and warehousing would not be appropriate in the context of a strategy to upgrade local skills levels;
- business support – focusing financial assistance, marketing, and advice on sectors which have a bias to low skills would not be appropriate;
- cluster development – focusing on the development of supply chains and skills provision for relatively low value added clusters would not connect to a need to develop local skill levels;
- land and property – land reclamation assembly and disposal; new building activity and the refurbishment of old buildings, should focus on and use activities which have a high skills component.

Any local strategy to generate employment, for example through the use of European Structural Adjustment Funds or government area based regeneration initiatives (like New Deal for Communities), needs to explicitly address the linkage between the types of jobs that they are seeking to create and the kinds of skills being envisaged. 'Mismatches' between the two will not only lead to the potential coexistence of structural unemployment and skill shortages and gaps, but to out-migration of people and/or employers.

Such a 'co-determination' of economic, employment and skills policies needs to operate at all levels of governance – European, national, regional and local (Campbell and Meadows, 2001). Such a 'joined up' approach also requires agencies to cooperate with each other and engage in meaningful partnership activity (Campbell and Percy-Smith, 2000; Carley et al, 2001). It also requires resources, in the form of funding streams, to be made more flexible in their application, as there are now, for example, under the Regional Development Agency 'single pot' arrangements and in New Deal for Communities areas. It also means that the strategies and plans of the various agencies, that operate across and between the levels of governance, need to be effectively coordinated.

Conclusions

There is a powerful and persuasive case for a skills revolution: a real step change in the levels of the workforce's attainment and participation in education and training. Such a skills revolution would bring significant economic and social benefits. It could:

- increase productivity
- improve competitiveness
- improve our relative economic performance
- reduce structural unemployment
- reduce skills shortages
- reduce skill gaps
- reduce social exclusion
- reduce income inequalities
- reduce regional and local disparities in income and employment.

These represent a range of very considerable potential benefits. Of course, a skills revolution would not be able, on its own, to fully address all of these issues. However, it can make an important contribution to each of them, and, if connected effectively to economic competitiveness and social inclusion policy, is likely to be able to make a significant contribution to enhanced social well-being.

We must 'learn to succeed'. But radically improving our skills base is not, on its own, enough to secure success. It is a necessary but not sufficient condition. It needs to be part of a wider strategy to renew the UK through economic policies which continue to enhance our competitive advantage: raise our productivity; stimulate innovation and enhance creativity, and which simultaneously foster greater social inclusion; reducing unemployment; increasing people's earnings; and modernising public services. Raising skill levels can make a major contribution to creating a successful and inclusive society – if we seize the opportunity to do so. As Camus observed, "it is better to light a candle than curse the darkness".

References

Ashton, D., Davies, B., Felstead, A. and Green, F. (1999) *Work skills in Britain*, Coventry: Centre on Skills, Knowledge and Organisational Performance, University of Warwick.

Ashton, D. and Green, F. (1996) *Education, training and the global economy*, Cheltenham: Edward Elgar.

Atkinson, J. and Spilsbury, M. (1993) *Basic skills and jobs: A report on the basic skills needed at work*, London: Adult Literacy and Basic Skills Unit.

Baldwin, S., Campbell, M., Johnson, S. and Walton, F. (2001) *The South Yorkshire skills audit*, Sheffield: South Yorkshire Learning and Skills Council.

Barratt, A. (1998) *Exploring the returns to continuing vocational training in enterprises*, CEDEFOP Panorama 83, Luxembourg: EUR-OP.

Berman, E., Bound, J. and Machin, S. (1998) 'Implications of skill-biased technological change: international evidence', *Quarterly Journal of Economics*, vol 113, no 4, pp 1245-80.

Blundell, R., Dearden, L. and Meghir, C. (1996) *The determinants of work related training in Britain*, London: Institute of Fiscal Studies.

Blundell, R., Dearden, L. and Meghir, C. (1999) 'Human capital investment: the returns from education and training to the individual, the firm and the economy', *Fiscal Studies*, vol 20, no 1, pp 1-23.

Booth, A.L. and Snower, D.J. (eds) (1996) *Acquiring skills: Market failures, their symptoms and policy responses*, Cambridge: Cambridge University Press.

Borghans, L. and de Grip, A. (eds) (2000) *The overeducated worker? The economics of skill utilization*, Cheltenham: Edward Elgar.

Bosworth, D. (1999) *Empirical evidence of management skills in the UK*, Skills Task Force Research Paper 18, Nottingham: DfEE.

Bosworth, D., Davies, R. and Wilson, R.A. (2001) *The extent, causes and implications of skill deficiencies: Econometric analysis*, IER Working Paper 42, Coventry: Institute for Employment Research, University of Warwick.

Brown, P., Green, A. and Lauder, H. (2001) *High skills. Globalisation, competitiveness, and skill formation*, Oxford: Oxford University Press.

Bynner, J. (2001) 'Adult participation and progression in education', in F. Coffield (ed) *What progress are we making with lifelong learning? The Evidence from research*, Newcastle: Department of Education, University of Newcastle, pp 51-62.

Bynner, J. and Parsons, S. (1997) *It doesn't get any better*, London: Basic Skills Agency.

Cabinet Office (2000) *Sharing the nation's prosperity: Economic, social and environmental conditions in the countryside*, London: Cabinet Office.

Cabinet Office (2001a) *In demand:Adult skills in the 21st century*, London: Cabinet Office.

Cabinet Office (2001b) *Ethnic minorities economic performance*, London, April.

Campbell, M. (1993) 'Local policies to beat long-term unemployment', *Local Government Studies*, vol 19, no 4, pp 505-18.

Campbell, M. (1995) *Learning pays: Individual commitment, learning and economic development*, Leeds: Policy Research Institute for DfEE, Leeds Metropolitan University.

Campbell, M. (2000) *Learning pays and learning works*, Sheffield: National Advisory Council for Education and Training Targets.

Campbell, M. (2001) *Skills in England 2001:The key messages*, London: DES.

Campbell, M. (2002) 'Skill rich, skill poor: local variations in skill levels', *Journal of Education and Training for Socio-economic Development*, vol 1, no 1.

Campbell, M., Baldwin, S., Chapman, R., Johnson, S., Upton, A. and Walton, F. (2001) *Skills in England 2001. The research report*, London: DES.

Campbell, M., Chapman, R. and Hutchinson, J. (1999) *Spatial skill variations: Their extent and implications*, Skill Task Force Research Paper 14, Nottingham: DfEE.

Campbell, M. and Meadows, P. (2001) *What works locally: Lessons on local employment policy*, York: Joseph Rowntree Foundation.

Campbell, M. and Percy-Smith, J. (2000) *Partnerships for success. A good practice guide*, London: DfEE.

Carley, M., Campbell, M., Kearns, A., Wood, M. and Young, R. (2001) *Regeneration in the 21st century: Policies into practice*, Bristol/York: The Policy Press for the Joseph Rowntree Foundation.

Chapman, P.G. (1993) *The economics of training*, LSE Handbooks in Economics, London: Harvester Wheatsheaf.

Coffield, F. (ed) (2001) *Speaking truth to power: Research and policy on lifelong learning*, Bristol: The Policy Press.

Coleman, S. and Keep, E. (2001) *Background literature review for PIU project on workforce development*, SKOPE mimeo, Coventry: Centre on Skills, Knowledge and Organisational Performance, University of Warwick.

Cosh, A. et al (2000) *The relationship between training and employment growth in small and medium sized enterprises*, Working Paper No 188, Cambridge: Centre for Business Research, University of Cambridge.

Coyle, D. (1999) *The weightless world: Strategies for managing the digital economy*, Oxford: Capstone.

Dearden, L., Macintosh, S., Myck, M. and Vignoles, A. (2001) *Basic skills, soft skills and labour market outcomes*, DfEE Research Report 250, Nottingham: DfES.

Dearden, L., Macintosh, S., Myck, M. and Vignoles, A. (2000) *The returns to academic vocational and basic skills in Britain*, DfEE Research Report 192, Nottingham: DfEE.

Dearden, L., Reed, H. and van Reenan, J. (2000) *Who gains when workers Train?*, Working Paper 00/04, London: Institute for Fiscal Studies.

DfES (Department for Education and Skills) (2001b) *Moving on*, September.

DfEE (Department for Education and Employment) (2000) *National learning targets for England for 2002*, Annual Report 2000, Sheffield: DfEE.

DfEE (1997) *National Adult Learning Survey*, Sheffield: DfEE.

DTI (Department of Trade and Industry) (2001) *UK competitiveness indicators* (2nd edn), London: DTI.

DWP (Department for Work and Pensions) (2001) *Opportunity for all: Review of progress*, Third Annual Report, London: DWP.

Englander, A.S. and Gurney, A. (1999) *Productivity in perspective*, OECD Observer Issue, 188, Paris: OECD.

Englander, A.S. and Gurney, A. (1994) *Productivity growth: Medium term trends*, Economic Studies 22, Paris: OECD

Felstead, A., Ashton, D., Burchell, B. and Green, F. (1999) 'Skill trends in Britain: trajectories over the past decade', in F. Coffield (ed) *Speaking truth to power: Research and policy on lifelong learning*, Bristol: The Policy Press, pp 55-72.

Felstead, A., Ashton, D. and Green, F. (2000) 'Are Britain's workplace skills becoming more unequal?', *Cambridge Journal of Economics*, vol 24, pp 709-27.

Finegold, D. (1991) 'Institutional incentives and skill creation: pre-conditions for a high skill equilibrium', in P. Ryan (ed) *International comparisons of vocational education and training for intermediate skills*, London: Falmer Press, pp 93-116.

Finegold, D. and Soskice, D. (1988) 'The failure of training in Britain: analysing and prescription', *Oxford Review of Economic Policy*, vol 4, no 3, pp 21-53.

Gallie, D. (1991) 'Patterns of Skill Change', *Work, Employment and Society*, vol 5, no 3, pp 319-51.

Green, A. and Owen, D. (2001) *Skills, local areas and unemployment*, Nottingham: DfEE.

Green, F. (1997) *Review of information on the benefits of training for employers*, Sheffield: DfEE.

Green, F. (1999) *The market value of generic skills*, Skills Task Force Research Paper 8, Sudbury: DfEE.

Green, F. and Steedman, H. (1997) *Into the 21st century: An assessment of British skill profiles and prospects*, London: London School of Economics and Political Science.

Green, F. et al (2002) *Work skills in Britain 1986-2001*, Nottingham: DfES.

Green, F., Felstead, A. and Gallie, D. (2002) *Work skills in Britain 2001*, Nottingham: DfES.

Green, F., Ashton, D., Burchell, B., Davies, B. and Felstead, A. (2000) 'Are British workers becoming more skilled?', in L. Borghans and A. de Grip (eds) *The overeducated worker? The economics of skill utilization*, Cheltenham: Edward Elgar, pp 77-106.

HEFCE (2001) *Supply and demand in higher education*, HEFCE: Bristol.

HM Treasury (2001) *Productivity in the UK: Enterprise and the productivity challenge*, London: HM Treasury.

Harmon, C. and Walker, I. (2001) *The returns to education: A review of evidence, issues and deficiencies in the literature*, DfEE Research Report 254, Nottingham: DfEE.

Haskel, J. and Martin, C. (1996) 'Skill shortages, productivity growth and wage inflation', in A.L. Booth and D.J. Snower (eds) *Acquiring skills: Market failures, their symptoms and policy responses*, pp 147-73.

Hillage, J., Uden, T., Aldridge, F. and Eccles, J. (2000) *Adult learning In England: A review*, Brighton: Institute for Employment Studies.

Hogarth, T. and Wilson, R. (2001) *The extent, causes and implications of skill deficiencies: Synthesis report*, IER Working Paper 37, Coventry: Institute for Employment Research, University of Warwick.

Hogarth, T., Wilson, R., Shury, J. and Vivian, D. (2001) *Employers skill survey 2001*, Nottingham: DfEE.

Johnson, S. (1999) *Skills issues in small and medium sized enterprises*, Skills Task Force Research Paper 13, Nottingham: DfEE.

Johnson, S., Campbell, M., Devins, D., Gold, G. and Hamblett, J. (2000) *Learning pays: The bottom line*, Sheffield: National Advisory Council for Education and Training Targets.

Johnson, S. and Winterton, J. (1999) *Management skills*, Skills Task Force Research Paper 3, London: DfEE.

Keep, E. and Mayhew, K. (1996) 'Evaluating the assumptions that underlie training policy', in A. Booth and D. Snower (eds) *Acquiring skills: Market failures, their symptons and policy responses*, Cambridge: Cambridge University Press.

Leadbeater, C. (2000) *Living on thin air: The new economy*, London: Viking.

Learning and Skills Council (2001) *Strategic framework to 2004: Corporate plan*, Coventry: Learning and Skills Council.

McNabb, R. and Whitfield, K. (eds) (1994) *The market for training: International perspectives on theory, methodology and policy*, Aldershot: Avebury.

Machin, S. and van Reenen, J. (1998) *Technology and changes in skill structure. Evidence from seven OECD countries*, Institute for Fiscal Studies Working Paper W98/4, London: Institute for Fiscal Studies.

Machin, S. and Vignoles, A (2001) 'The economic benefits of training to the individual, the firm and the economy: the key issues', Paper prepared for the Cabinet Office Workforce Development Project, London: Centre for the Economics of Education.

Manncorda, M. and Robinson, P. (1997) 'Unskilled or overqualified? Qualifications, occupations and earnings in the British labour market', Paper presented to the Lower Conference, Centre for Economic Performance, London School of Economics and Political Science, 12-13 December.

Mason, G., van Ark, B. and Wagner, K. (1994) 'Productivity, product quality and workforce skills: food processing in four European countries', *National Institute Economic Review.*

Mason, G., van Ark, B. and Wagner, K. (1996) 'Workforce skills, product quality and economic performance', in A.L. Booth and D.J. Snower (eds) *Acquiring skills: Market failures, their symptoms and policy responses*, pp 175-97.

Metcalf, H., Walling, A. and Fogarty, M. (1994) *Individual commitment to learning: Employer attitudes*, Research Series 40, Sheffield: DfEE.

Moser, Sir C. (1999) *A fresh start: Improving literacy and numeracy*, Sudbury: DfEE.

NACETT (National Advisory Council for Education and Training Targets) (2000) *Aiming higher. NACETT's report on the National Learning Targets for England and Advice on Targets Beyond 2002*, Sheffield: NACETT.

National Skills Task Force (1999) *Delivering skills for all: Second report of the National Skills Task Force*, Sudbury: DfEE.

National Skills Task Force (2000) *Skills for all: Research report for the National Skills Task Force*, Sudbury: DfEE.

O'Connell, P.J. (1999) *Adults in training: An international comparison of continuing education and training*, Paris: OECD.

O'Mahony, M., Wagner, K. and Paulsen, M. (1994) *Changing fortunes: An industry study of British and German productivity growth over three decades*, NIESR Report Series 7, London: National Institute of Economic and Social Research.

OECD (Organisation for Economic Co-operation and Development) (2001d) *The well-being of nations: The role of human and social capital*, Paris: OECD.

OECD (2001c) *Cities and regions in the new learning economy*, Paris: OECD.

OECD (2001a) *Education at a glance: OECD indicators*, 2001 Edition, Paris: OECD.

OECD (2001b) *Education policy analysis*, Paris: OECD.

OECD (2000) *Education at a glance: OECD indicators*, 2000 Edition, Paris: OECD.

OECD and Statistics Canada (2000) *Literacy in the information age*, Paris: OECD.

OECD (1999) *Employment outlook*, Paris: OECD.

OECD (1998) *Human capital investment: An international comparison*, Paris: OECD.

Oulton, N. (1996) *Competition and the dispersion of labour productivity amongst UK companies*, National Institute of Economic and Social Research Discussion Paper 103, National Institute of Economic and Social Research, London.

Owen, D., Green, A., Pitcher, J. and Maguire, M. (2000) *Minority ethnic participation and achievements in education, training and the labour market*, DfEE Research Report 225, Nottingham: DfEE.

Patterson, M.G., West, M.A. and Lawthom, R. (1997) *Impact of people management practices on business performance*, Issues in People Management, 22, London: Institute of Personnel and Development.

Percy-Smith, J. (2000) *Policy responses to social exclusion: Towards inclusion?*, Buckingham: Open University Press.

Prais, S.J. (1995) *Productivity, education and training: An international perspective*, Cambridge: Cambridge University Press.

Psacharopoulos, E. (1985) *Returns to education: A further international update and implication,* Journal of Human Resources, vol 20, no 4, pp 583-604.

Reich, R. (1993) *The work of nations: Preparing ourselves for 21st century capitalism*, London: Simon & Schuster.

Reich, R. (1998) *Locked in the cabinet*, New York, NY: Vantage.

Sargant, N. (2000) *The learning divide revisited: A report of the findings of a UK-wide survey on adult participation in education and learning*, Leicester: National Institute of Adult Continuing Education.

Sianasi, B. and van Reenan, J. (2000) *The returns to education: A review of the macroeconomic literature*, Centre for Economics of Education Discussion Paper 6, London: Centre for Economics of Education, London School of Economics and Political Science.

Snower, D.J. (1996) 'The low-skill, bad-job trap', in A.L. Booth and D.J. Snower (eds) *Acquiring skills: market failures, their symptoms and policy responses*, pp 109-24.

Social Exclusion Unit (1998) *A national strategy for neighbourhood renewal*, London: Cabinet Office.

Spilsbury, D. (2001) *Learning and training at work 2000*, DfEE Research Report 269, Nottingham: DfEE.

Sturm, R. (1993) *How do education and training affect a country's economic performance? A literature survey*, Santa Monica, CA: Institute on Education and Training.

Thurow, L.C. (1999) *Creating wealth: The new rules for individuals, companies and countries in a knowledge-based economy*, London: Nicholas Brearley.

Wilson, R.A. (2001a) *Projections of occupations and qualifications 2000/2001*, vol 1, UK Results, Sheffield: DfES.

Wilson, R.A. (2001b) *Projections of occupations and qualifications 2000/2001*, vol 2, Regional Results, Sheffield: DfES.

Wood, A. (1995) 'How trade hurt unskilled workers', *Journal of Economic Perspectives*, vol 9, no 3, pp 57-80.

Index

Page references for figures and tables are indicated by *italics*

V

van Ark, B. 74
van Reenan, J. 45, 77
Vignoles, A. 72
Voltaire 95

W

wage premium *see* earnings
Walker, I. 70
Walsall 77
Warwick Institute for Employment
    Research (WIER) 25, 29, 32
Wells, H.G. 7
West Midlands
    employment sectors 47
    participation rates 19, 20, *20*
    qualifications 18, 54, *55*, 78
    skill gaps 31
Whitfield, K. 74
wholesale and retail
    skill gaps 30, 86
    skills shortages 27, *28*
Wilson, R.A. 25-6, 32, *48*, *50*, 51, 52, *53*,
    54, *55*, 56, 59
Winterton, J. 30
women
    earnings and qualifications 68, 69
    employment 48-9
    occupational change 52, *53*
    participation rates *15*, 16
    qualifications *9*, 10
    skill levels 62
    training and earnings 72
Wood, A. 45
work organisation 45
workforce qualifications *see* qualifications
workplace training *see* training

Y

Yorkshire and Humberside
    employment sectors 47
    participation rates *20*
    qualifications 54, *55*
    see also Humberside; North Yorkshire;
        South Yorkshire
young people
    participation rates 12-13, *13*, 84, 88
    qualifications 8, 33, 35
    skill levels 33, 62

Also available from The Policy Press

Creating a learning society?
Learning careers and policies for lifelong learning
Stephen Gorard and Gareth Rees, School of Social Sciences, Cardiff University

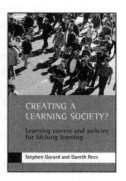

"... should have a considerable impact in Britain and elsewhere." John Field, Department of Continuing Education, University of Warwick
PB £17.99 US$32.50 ISBN 1 86134 286 1
HB £50.00 US$90.00 ISBN 1 86134 393 0

The ESRC Learning Society Series

Edited by Frank Coffield, Department of Education, University of Newcastle upon Tyne

Differing visions of a Learning Society
Research findings Volume 1
PB £18.99 US$34.50 ISBN 1 86134 230 6
HB £45.00 US$81.00 ISBN 1 86134 246 2

Differing visions of a Learning Society
Research findings Volume 2
PB £15.99 US$28.75 ISBN 1 86134 247 0
HB £45.00 US$81.00 ISBN 1 86134 248 9

"Volumes 1 and 2 are timely, important and definitely to be recommended." British Educational Research Journal

These two volumes, the fruit of a major research programme funded by the ESRC, make an important contribution to the public debate on lifelong learning and are essential reading for policy makers, practitioners, academics and researchers.

More titles overleaf

The Learning Society and people with learning difficulties

Sheila Riddell, Strathclyde Centre for Disability Research, Stephen Baron, Faculty of Education and Alastair Wilson, Strathclyde Centre for Disability Research, University of Glasgow

"A joy to read ... combines theoretical and policy analysis within a framework that is informed by a broad political awareness." Widening Participation and Lifelong Learning
PB £17.99 US$32.50 ISBN 1 86134 223 3

Adult guidance services and The Learning Society
Emerging policies in the European Union

Will Bartlett, School for Policy Studies, University of Bristol, Teresa Rees, School of Social Sciences, Cardiff University and A.G. Watts, National Institute for Careers Education and Counselling

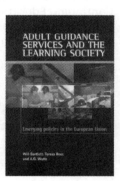

"... a well-written and interesting book, bringing together a useful range of material to stimulate debate about how best to develop adult guidance." British Journal of Guidance & Counselling
PB £14.99 US$26.99 ISBN 1 86134 153 9

For further information about these and other titles published by The Policy Press, please visit our website at: www.policypress.org.uk or telephone +44 (0)117 954 6800

To order, please contact:
Marston Book Services
PO Box 269
Abingdon
Oxon OX14 4YN
UK
Tel: +44 (0)1235 465500
Fax: +44 (0)1235 465556
E-mail: direct-orders@marston.co.uk